Collins Primary Maths
Answer Book

3

Series Editor: Peter Clarke

Authors: Andrew Edmondson, Elizabeth Jurgenson,
Jeanette Mumford, Sandra Roberts

Published by Collins Educational
An imprint of HarperCollins*Publishers* Ltd
77–85 Fulham Palace Road
Hammersmith
London
W6 8JB
www.**Collins**Educational.com

First published 2000

ISBN 000 711705 1

Cover design by Susi Martin and Jacqueline Palmer

Cover illustration by Jan Lewis

Series design by Sylvia Tate

Text page design by Ken Vail Graphic Design

Contents

Pupil Book 1 5

Pupil Book 2 18

Pupil Book 3 27

Support Copymasters 37

Extension Copymasters 47

Homework Copymasters 52

Answers

Pupil Book 1

Autumn

Week 1, Lesson 1 – Page 5

Refresher

1 a fifty nine, twenty six, forty four
b seven, eighty four, eighteen
c sixty two, thirty, ninety one
d twenty, sixty two, fifty

2 59 This number has 5 tens
7 This number has 0 tens
62 This number has 6 tens
20 This number has 2 tens

3 26 This number has 6 units
84 This number has 4 units
30 This number has 0 units
62 This number has 2 units

4 a 8 **b** 0 **c** 25 **d** 74 **e** 12

Practice

1 a four hundred and ninety-two, three hundred and eighty-two, five hundred and seventeen
b four hundred and thirty-one, one hundred and ninety-three, three hundred and eighty
c nine hundred and three, three hundred, two hundred and one
d two hundred and sixty-seven, nine hundred and ninety-six, seventy-five

2 492 This number has 9 tens
431 This number has 3 tens
903 This number has 0 tens
267 This number has 6 tens

3 382 This number has 2 units
193 This number has 3 units
300 This number has 0 units
996 This number has 6 units

4 517 This number has 5 hundreds
380 This number has 3 hundreds
201 This number has 2 hundreds
75 This number has 0 hundreds

5 a 745 **b** 966 **c** 555
d 417 **e** 611

Week 1, Lesson 2 – Page 6

Answers will vary

Week 1, Lesson 3 – Page 7

Refresher

1 a 11 cm **b** 8 cm **c** 160 cm **d** 80 cm

2 a 10 cm **b** 7 cm **c** 5 cm
d 4 cm **e** 0 cm

Practice

1 a 12 cm **b** 4 cm **c** 200 cm **d** 100 cm
e 200 cm **f** 200 cm **g** 4 m **h** 3 m

Week 2, Lesson 1 – Page 8

Refresher

10 + **1** = 11 9 + **2** = 11 **8** + 3 = 11
7 + **4** = 11 **6** + 5 = **11**

1 + 11 = 12 2 + **10** = 12 **3** + 9 = 12
4 + **8** = 12 5 + **7** = 12 **6** + **6** = 12

Practice

1 a 17 + 0 = 17 16 + 1 = 17 15 + 2 = 17
14 + 3 = 17 13 + 4 = 17 12 + 5 = 17
11 + 6 = 17 10 + 7 = 17 9 + 8 = 17
b 20 + 0 = 20 19 + 1 = 20 18 + 2 = 20
17 + 3 = 20 16 + 4 = 20 15 + 5 = 20
14 + 6 = 20 13 + 7 = 20 12 + 8 = 20
11 + 9 = 20 10 + 10 = 20

2 a 19 + 0 = 19 18 + 1 = 19 17 + 2 = 19
16 + 3 = 19 15 + 4 = 19 14 + 5 = 19
13 + 6 = 19 12 + 7 = 19 11 + 8 = 19
10 + 9 = 19
b 16 + 0 = 16 15 + 1 = 16 14 + 2 = 16
13 + 3 = 16 12 + 4 = 16 11 + 5 = 16
10 + 6 = 16 9 + 7 = 16

Week 2, Lesson 2 – Page 9

Refresher

1 a 15 b 15 c 12
d 17 e 14 f 13

2 a 25 + 8 = **33** b 27+5 = **32**
c 23 + 9 = **32** d 26+7 = **33**
e 29 + 3 = **32** f 29+9 = **38**

Practice

Answers will differ

Week 2, Lesson 3 – Page 10

Refresher

1 a 15 – 4 = **11** b 14 – 5 = **9**
c 11 – 3 = **8** d 17 – 8 = **9**
e 13 – 7 = **6** f 19 – 6 = **13**
g 18 – 7 = **11** h 12 – 6 = **6**
i 20 – 9 = **11** j 16 – 5 = **11**

Practice

1 Answers will vary e.g.
53 – 8 = 45 31 – 9 = 22
24 – 4 = 20 73 – 6 = 67
42 – 5 = 37

Week 2, Lesson 4 – Page 11

Refresher

1 a 11 + 10 = **21** b 6 + 7 = **13**
c 4 + 5 = **9** d 3 + 2 = **5**
e 14 + 15 = **29** f 21 + 20 = **41**

Practice

a 8 + 9 = **17** b 31 + 33 = **64**
c 9 + 10 = **19** d 43 + 39 = **82**
e 102 + 98 = **200** f 21 + 19 = **40**
g 22 + 19 = **41** h 73 + 69 = **142**
i 11 + 13 = **24** j 64 + 61 = **125**
k 4 + 6 = **10** l 89 + 89 = **178**

Week 2, Lesson 5 – Page 12

Refresher

1 a 14 + 10 = **24** **24** + 3 = **27**
14 + 13 = **27**
b 14 – 10 = **4** **4** – 3 = **1**
14 – 13 = **1**

2 a 16 + 12 = 28 16 – 12 = 4
b 15 + 13 = 28 15 – 13 = 2
c 26 + 24 = 50 26 – 24 = 2
d 20 + 12 = 32 20 – 12 = 8
e 17 + 11 = 28 17 – 11 = 6

Practice

1 a 54 + 16 = 70 54 – 16 = 38
b 36 + 12 = 48 36 – 12 = 24
c 46 + 22 = 68 46 – 22 = 24
d 69 + 21 = 90 69 – 21 = 48
e 57 + 33 = 90 57 + 33 = 24
f 85 + 15 = 100 85 – 15 = 70
g 39 + 32 = 71 39 – 32 = 7
h 67 + 15 = 82 67 – 15 = 52

Week 3, Lesson 1 – Page 13

Refresher

1 Answers will vary e.g.
42 + 15 = 57 23 + 12 = 35
30 + 32 = 62

2 Answers will vary e.g.
28 – 13 = 15 19 – 12 = 7
29 – 14 = 15

Practice

1 e.g.
25 + 47 = 72 64 + 13 = 77
82 + 57 = 139 78 – 13 = 65
64 – 47 = 17 82 – 25 = 57

Week 3, Lesson 2 – Page 14

Refresher

1 a 50p b £1 c £1
d £2 e £2 f £1
g £2 h £2 i £1

Practice

1 a £10 b £10 c £5
d £5 e £20 f £20

2 £15

3 £40

4 £35

Week 3, Lesson 3 – Page 15

Refresher

1 a £1.10 **b** £1.20 **c** £1.50
d £1.90 **e** £2.70 **f** £2.45
g £6.01 **h** £5.95 **i** £3.43

Practice

1

What I bought	£.p.	p
Sweets	£1·10	110p
Crisps	£4.65	465p
Cinema	£3·20	320p
Books	£6·08	608p
Bus fares	£1.65	165p
Comics	£2.05	205p
Games	£2.36	236p
Clothes	£8·61	861p

2 a £3.70 **b** £5.75 **c** £11.81

Week 3, Lesson 4 – Page 16

Refresher

1 a 90p **b** 90p
c £1.40 **d** 75p 25p

Practice

1 a 75p **b** 1 week
c £1.25 **d** 50p + 20p + 10p + 5p

Week 3, Lesson 5 – Page 17

Refresher

1 a 40 **b** 48 33 **c** 17 **d** 15

Practice

1 a 2 **b** 4 **c** 92 **d** £64

Week 4, Lesson 1 – Page 18

Refresher

a 10 minutes past 5
b 15 minutes past 8
c 5 minutes past 11
d 25 minutes past 12
e 15 minutes to 12
f 10 minutes to 9
g 20 minutes to 3
h 5 minutes to 6

Practice

1 a The time is **25** minutes **to** 3.
b In another **10** minutes it will be $\frac{1}{4}$ to 3.
c In 25 minutes it will be **3 o'clock**.
2 a 10 minutes past 10
b 10 o'clock
c 20 minutes past 8
3 Open

Week 4, Lesson 2 – Page 19

Refresher

1 a 10 cm **b** 9 cm **c** 12 cm

Practice

1 a > 18 cm **b** < 11 cm **c** = 8 cm
d = 10 cm **e** > 7 cm **f** > 11 cm

Week 4, Lesson 3 – Page 20

Refresher

Open

Practice

1 a 5.5 cm **b** 4.5 cm **c** 2.5 cm
d 6.5 cm
2 e 1.5 cm **f** 3.5 cm **g** 8.5 cm
h 9.5 cm **i** 7.5 cm
3 7.5 cm

Week 4, Lesson 4 – Page 21

Refresher

1 Answers will vary
2 a 4.5 cm **b** 5 cm **c** 2.5 cm
d 3 cm **e** 1 cm **f** 3.5 cm

Practice

Open

Week 4, Lesson 5 – Page 22

Refresher

Open

Practice

1 a 11.5 cm **b** 11.5 cm
c 6.5 cm **d** 2.5 cm
e 7 cm **f** 13 cm

g 4.5 cm h 7.5 cm

2 a Open b Open

Week 5, Lesson 1 – Page 23

Refresher

1 A fits envelope 2 B fits envelope 1

C fits envelope 4 D fits envelope 3

Practice

1 2m 80 cm

2 a 99 cm b 9 cm

3 a 5.5 cm b 9 cm

4 14 m

5 Yes

Week 5, Lesson 2 – Page 24

Refresher

solid	picture number
a	5
b	8
c	1
d	2
e	6
f	3
g	9
h	7

Practice

a

prism	not a prism
cube	cylinder
cuboid	cone
hexagonal prism	sphere
triangular prism	hemisphere

b

prism	not a prism
wedge cheese	tin soup
cube tissues	cornetto
wash tabs	Terry's Orange
Toblerone	$\frac{1}{2}$ melon
packet tea	
hexagonal box	

Week 5, Lesson 3 – Page 25

Refresher

1 a I am a **cube / cuboid**

b I am a **cylinder**

Practice

shape a – hexagonal prism

shape b – hemisphere

shape c – square base prism / cuboid

shape d – triangular prism

shape e – sphere

Week 5, Lesson 4 – Page 26

Refresher

2 Shapes **b, d, e, h** are squares because each shape has **4** equal sides and **4** right angle **vertices**.

Practice

Pattern as shown on pupil page

Week 5, Lesson 5 – Page 27

Refresher

Shape	Four-sided	Curved side
A	✗	✓
C	✓	✗
B	✓	✗
D	✗	✓

Practice

Shape	Four-sided	Sides same length
B	✓	✗
A	✗	✗
C	✓	✗
D	✗	✓

Shape	Five vertices	1 or more right angles
D	✓	✓
A	✓	✓
B	✗	✓
C	✗	✗

Week 6, Lesson 1 – Page 28

Refresher

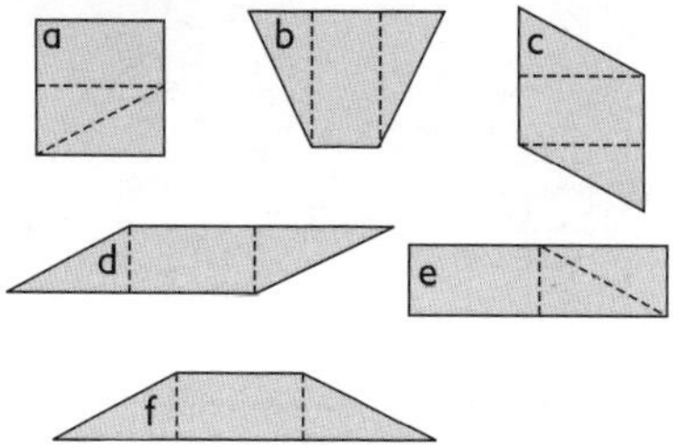

a, e

Practice

1

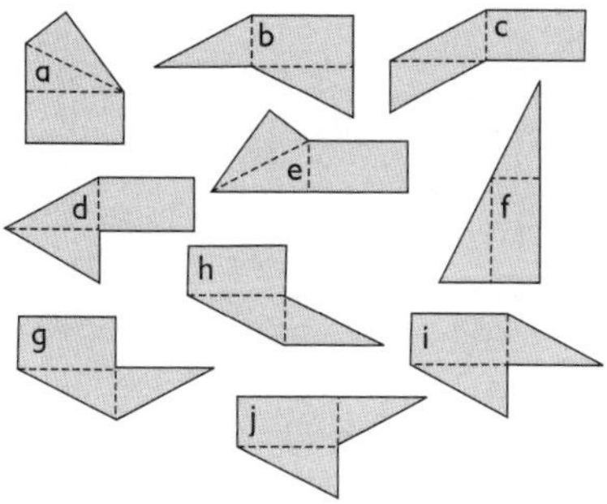

2

Property	letter of shape
a with 1 right angle	b, f, i, j
b with more than 1 right angle	a, c, d, e, g, h

Week 6, Lesson 2 – Page 29

Refresher

1 a Rob–**B1** b Amy–**A3**
c Charlie–**C3** d Anna–**A2**

2 a B3 b C2 c A1

Practice

1 a Ryan b Luke c Ella
d Lucy e Liam f Emma

2 a A5 b C4 c A3
d D1 e B1 f C3
g C1 h D2

Week 6, Lesson 3 – Page 30

Refresher

a E2
b B2
c F5
d B4
e B5

Practice

1 a boat hire
b banana trees
c adventure park
d sailing boat
e beach
f lake

2 a E2 to D2 to **C2** to **C3** to **C4** to **B4** to B5
b E2 to **E3** to **D3**

Week 7, Lesson 1 – Page 31

Refresher

Open

Practice

1 b 6 groups
3 in each group
6×3 = 18

c 4 groups
4 in each group
4×4 = 16

d 3 groups
12 in each group
12×3 = 36

e 5 groups
6 in each group
6×5 = 30

f 7 groups
10 in each group
7×10 = 70

2 Answers will differ

Week 7, Lesson 2 – Page 32

Refresher

1 a 42, 52, 62, **72**, **82**, **92**, **102**
b 7, 17, 27, **37**, **47**, **57**, **67**
c 8, 18, **28**, 38, **48**, **58**, **68**
d 26, 36, 46, **56**, **66**, **76**, **86**
e 32, 42, 52, **62**, **72**, **82**, **92**

Practice

1a	**10**	20	**30**
b	**27**	37	**47**
c	**100**	200	**300**
d	**375**	475	**575**
2a	85	75	
	65	55	
	45	35	
	25		
b	82	72	62
	52	42	
	32	22	
c	800	700	
	600	500	
	400	300	
	200		
d	747	647	547
	447	347	
	247	147	
e	851	751	
	651	551	
	451	351	
	251		

Week 7, Lesson 3 – Page 33

Refresher

1a	2 → 4	4 → 6	8 → 10
	12 → 14	16 → 18	20 → 22
b	20 → 18	16 → 14	12 → 10
	8 → 6	4 → 2	2 → 0
c	7 → 9	11 → 13	15 → 17
	9 → 11	13 → 15	19 → 21
d	21 → 19	17 → 15	13 → 11
	5 → 3	19 → 17	15 → 13

Practice

1a 12, 14, 16, **18**, **20**, **22**, **24**, **26**
b 33, 35, 37, **39**, **41**, **43**, **45**, **47**
c 26, 24, 22, **20**, **18**, **16**, **14**, **12**
d 80, 78, 76, **74**, **72**, **70**, **68**, **66**
e 75, 77, 79, **81**, **83**, **85**, **87**, **89**
f **100**, **98**, 96, **94**, **92**, 90, **88**, **86**

Practice

2

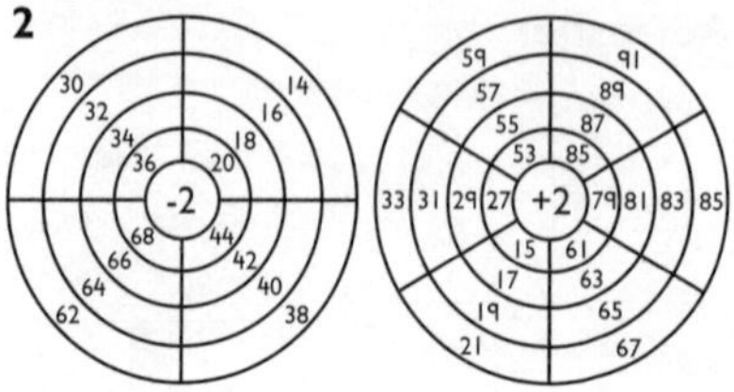

Week 7, Lesson 4 – Page 34

Refresher

1a even
b **7** – odd
c **17** – odd
d **16** – even
e **22** – even
f **19** – odd
g **31** – odd

Practice

1a odd – 89, 51, 73, 23, 27, 45, 37
even – 74, 50, 62
b odd – 25, 71, 69, 11, 1
even – 36, 26, 70, 96, 60
c odd – 97, 49, 43, 37
even – 62, 72, 76, 24, 58, 12
d odd – 137, 181, 211, 7
even – 94, 316, 194, 114, 46, 100

2 Open

Week 7, Lesson 5 – Page 35

Refresher

1a 2 + 2 = **4**	**b** 4 + 6 = **10**
c 10 + 10 = **20**	**d** 4 + 4 = **8**
e 8 + 4 = **12**	**f** 10 + 4 = **14**
g 6 + 6 = **12**	**h** 8 + 6 = **14**
i 10 + 8 = **18**	
2a 5 + 5 = **10**	**b** 9 + 9 = **18**
c 11 + 9 = **20**	**d** 7 + 7 = **14**
e 3 + 5 = **8**	**f** 11 + 7 = **18**
g 3 + 3 = **6**	**h** 7 + 9 = **16**
i 13 + 3 = **16**	

Practice

1 Yes

2 Odd + Even = Odd

Week 8, Lesson 1 – Page 36

Refresher

1 a 4 + 4 = **8**
  b 3 + 3 + 3 + 3 = **12**
  c 5 + 5 + 5 = **15**
  d 2 + 2 + 2 + 2 + 2 = **10**
  Content of pictures will vary

2 a 2×4 = **8** b 4×3 = **12**
  c 3×5 = **15** d 5×2 = **10**

3 They contain the same number of groups, and the same number in each group.
  The answers are the same.

Practice

1 a 3 + 3 + 3 + 3 = **12**
  4×3 = **12**
  b 5+5+5+5+5=**25**
  5×5 = **25**
  c 6 + 6 = **12**
  2×6 = **12**
  d 3 + 3 + 3 + 3 + 3 + 3 = **18**
  6×3 = **18**
  e 4 + 4 + 4 = **12**
  3×4 = **12**
  f 6 + 6 + 6 + 6 = **24**
  4×6 = **24**

2 a 2×5 = 10 b 8×5 = 40
  5×2 = 10 5×8 = 40
  c 6×1 = 6 d 3×4 = 12
  1×6 = 6 4×3 = 12

Week 8, Lesson 2 – Page 37

Refresher

1 a 5, 10, 15, **20**, **25**, **30**, **35**, **40**, **45**
  b 2, 4, **6**, 8, **10**, 12, **14**, **16**, **18**
  c 10, 20, **30**, **40**, **50**, **60**, 70, **80**, **90**

Practice

1 a 2×2 = **4** 3×2 = **6**
  10×2 = **20** 9×2 = **18**
  b 1×2 = **2** 4×2 = **8**
  8×2 = **16** 7×2 = **14**
  c 5×2 = **10** 6×2 = **12**
  11×2 = **22** 0×2 = **0**

2 a 10×5 = **50** 9×5 = **45**
  2×5 = **10** 3×5 = **15**
  b 5×5 = **25** 4×5 = **20**
  6×5 = **30** 7×5 = **35**
  c 1×5 = **5** 8×5 = **40**
  0×5 = **0** 11×5 = **55**

3 a 2×10 = **20** 5×10 = **50**
  1×10 = **10**
  b 4×10 = **40** 6×10 = **60**
  10×10 = **100**
  c 7×10 = **70** 3×10 = **30**
  8×10 = **80**

Week 8, Lesson 3 – Page 38

Refresher

1

Number of jumps	1	2	3	4	5	6	7	8	9	10
Landing number	3	6	9	12	15	18	21	24	27	30

2 1×3 = 3 2×3 = 6
  3×3 = 9 4×3 = 12
  5×3 = 15 6×3 = 18
  7×3 = 21 8×3 = 24
  9×3 = 27 10×3 = 30

Practice

1 a 2×3 = **6** 5×3 = **15**
  10×3 = **30** 1×3 = **3**
  b 4×3 = **12** 7×3 = **21**
  3×3 = **9** 9×3 = **27**
  c 6×3 = **18** 0×3 = **0**
  8×3 = **24** 11×3 = **33**
  d **5**×3 = 15 **10**×3 = 30
  3×3 = 9 **1**×3 = 3
  e 3×**4** = 12 3×**9** = 27
  8×3 = 24 **2**×3 = 6
  f 3×**7** = 21 3×**6** = 18
  3×3 = 9 **11**×**3** = 33

Week 8, Lesson 4 – Page 39

Refresher

1 a $3\times2=6$
I spend 6p

b $9\times3=27$
They cost 27p

c $10\times3=30$
They cost 30p

d $3\times5=15$
I spend 15p

e $4\times3=12$
They cost 12p

f $7\times3=21$
No

Practice

1 a $8\times3=24$
24 leaves altogether

b $5\times3=15$
They have 15 new tennis balls

c $4\times3=12$
£12 for 3 bunches

d $2\times3=6$
He needs 6 wickets

e $6\times3=18$
There are 18 wheels altogether

f $3\times10=30$
There are 30 cakes altogether

2 a $7\times3=\mathbf{21}$ b $3\times4=\mathbf{12}$
c $3\times2=\mathbf{6}$ d $5\times3=\mathbf{15}$

Week 8, Lesson 5 – Page 40

Refresher

1 Open

2 $1\times4=4$ $2\times4=8$
$3\times4=12$ $4\times4=16$
$5\times4=20$ $6\times4=24$
$7\times4=28$ $8\times4=32$
$9\times4=36$ $10\times4=40$

Practice

1 a $5\times4=\mathbf{20}$ $2\times4=\mathbf{8}$
$10\times4=\mathbf{40}$ $1\times4=\mathbf{4}$

b $4\times4=\mathbf{16}$ $7\times4=\mathbf{28}$
$6\times4=\mathbf{24}$ $0\times4=\mathbf{0}$

c $3\times4=\mathbf{12}$ $9\times4=\mathbf{36}$
$8\times4=\mathbf{32}$ $11\times4=\mathbf{44}$

2 $5\times4=20$ $6\times4=24$ $4\times4=16$
$4\times5=20$ $4\times6=24$ $4\times4=16$

Week 9, Lesson 1 – Page 41

Refresher

1 a $6\times4=24$
£24

b $10\times4=40$
£40

c $5\times4=20$
£20

d $3\times4=12$
£12

e $4\times4=16$
£16

f $2\times4=8$
£8

Practice

1 a £16 is spent
b She spends £36
c The total cost is £32
d They spend £28
e He can buy 10 toys
f They spend £24 altogether

Week 9, Lesson 2 – Page 42

Refresher

1 a $4+4=8$
$2\times4=8$

b $10+10=20$
$2\times10=20$

c $5+5=10$
$2\times5=10$

d $7+7=14$
$2\times7=14$

e $6+6=12$
$2\times6=12$

f $2+2=4$
$2\times2=4$

g $8+8=16$
$2\times8=16$

h $9+9=18$
$2\times9=18$

i $11+11=22$
$2\times11=22$

Practice

1 a $5\times2=10$ $7\times2=14$
$10\times2=20$

b $11\times2=22$ $4\times2=8$
$15\times2=30$

c $6\times2=12$ $16\times2=32$
$13\times2=26$

2 a $20+20=40$ $11+11=22$
$15+15=30$

b $13+13=26$ $8+8=16$
$19+19=38$

c $7+7=14$ $18+18=36$
$10+10=20$

Week 9, Lesson 3 – Page 43

Refresher

1 1 + 1 = 2 | 3 + 3 = 6
5 + 5 = 10 | 7 + 7 = 14
9 + 9 = 18 | 2 + 2 = 4
4 + 4 = 8 | 6 + 6 = 12
8 + 8 = 16 | 10 + 10 = 20

2 6 + 6 = 12 | 8 + 8 = 16
60 + 60 = 120 | 80 + 80 = 160
7 + 7 = 14 | 4 + 4 = 8
70 + 70 = 140 | 40 + 40 = 80
2 + 2 = 4 | 1 + 1 = 2
20 + 20 = 40 | 100 + 100 = 200
3 + 3 = 6 | 5 + 5 = 10
30 + 30 = 60 | 50 + 50 = 100
9 + 9 = 18
90 + 90 = 180

Practice

15 + 15 = 30 | 95 + 95 = 190
60 + 60 = 120 | 25 + 25 = 50
80 + 80 = 160 | 45 + 45 = 90
55 + 55 = 110 | 100 + 100 = 200
85 + 85 = 170 | 75 + 75 = 150
50 + 50 = 100 | 30 + 30 = 60

Week 9, Lesson 4 – Page 44

Refresher

1	10	100
2	20	200
3	30	300
4	40	400
5	50	500
6	60	600
7	70	700
8	80	800
9	90	900
10	100	1000

Practice

1 a 3×10 = 30 **b** 6×10 = 60
c 14×10 = 140 **d** 5×100 = 500
e 7×100 = 700 **f** 25×100 = 2500

Week 9, Lesson 5 – Page 45

Refresher

1 6 (×5) **30** 3 (×5) **15**
9 (×5) **45** 4 (×5) **20**
8 (×2) **16** 7 (×2) **14**
6 (×2) **12** 9 (×2) **18**
3 (×4) **12** 5 (×4) **20**
8 (×4) **32** 6 (×4) **24**
7 (×10) **70** 5 (×10) **50**
3 (×10) **30** 8 (×10) **80**
6 (×3) **18** 9 (×3) **27**
7 (×3) **21** 3 (×3) **9**

Practice

1 a £30 **b** £21 **c** 5
d £90 **e** 5 **f** £45

2 a 5×10 = 50
3×3 = 9
4×4 = 16
(50 + 9 + 16 = 75)
It costs £75 altogether

b 7×3 = 21
2×4 = 8
21 + 8 = 29
Yes

Week 10, Lesson 1 – Page 46

Refresher

1 a 2 **b** 1 **c** 3
2 a 3 **b** 2 **c** 4 **d** 5
3 a 2 **b** 4 **c** 3 **d** 5

Practice

1 a quarter **b** half
c half **d** three quarters

2 a $\frac{3}{4}$ **b** $\frac{1}{2}$
c $\frac{1}{2}$ **d** $\frac{1}{4}$

3 a Half of 10 is 5
b A quarter of 8 is 2
c Half of 20 is 10
d A quarter of 16 is 4
e Three quarters of 20 is 15

Week 10, Lesson 2 – Page 47

Refresher

1 a 5 **b** 1 **c** 3 **d** 2 **e** 4

2 a 1 **b** 2 **c** 3 **d** 4

Practice

1 a one third **b** three quarters
c half **d** two thirds
e quarter **f** half
g two thirds

2 a $\frac{2}{3}$ **b** $\frac{1}{4}$ **c** $\frac{1}{2}$ **d** $\frac{1}{3}$
e $\frac{3}{4}$ **f** $\frac{1}{2}$ **g** $\frac{1}{3}$

3 Answers will vary

Week 10, Lesson 3 – Page 48

Refresher

1 a $\frac{1}{4}$ of 8 = 2 **b** $\frac{1}{3}$ of 12 = 4
c $\frac{1}{5}$ of 10 = 2 **d** $\frac{1}{4}$ of 16 = 4
e $\frac{1}{5}$ of 15 = 3 **f** $\frac{1}{5}$ of 20 = 4

Practice

1 Answers will vary

2 a $\frac{1}{3}$ of 15 = 5 **b** $\frac{1}{4}$ of 16 = 4
c $\frac{1}{5}$ of 15 = 3 **d** $\frac{2}{3}$ of 12 = 8
e $\frac{3}{4}$ of 20 = 15 **f** $\frac{2}{5}$ of 30 = 12
g $\frac{3}{5}$ of 25 = 15 **h** $\frac{4}{5}$ of 20 = 16

Week 10, Lesson 4 – Page 49

Refresher

1 a $\frac{1}{10}$ **b** three tenths
c $\frac{6}{10}$ **d** nine tenths

2

	Apple	Orange
a	$\frac{1}{2}$	$\frac{1}{2}$
b	$\frac{1}{4}$	$\frac{3}{4}$
c	$\frac{3}{5}$	$\frac{2}{5}$
d	$\frac{2}{5}$	$\frac{3}{5}$
e	$\frac{3}{4}$	$\frac{1}{4}$
f	$\frac{4}{10}$	$\frac{6}{10}$

3 a $\frac{4}{10}$ **b** $\frac{2}{10}$
c $\frac{9}{10}$ **d** $\frac{1}{10}$
e $\frac{5}{10}$ or $\frac{1}{2}$

Practice

1 $\frac{1}{4}, \frac{1}{5}, \frac{2}{3}, \frac{3}{10}, \frac{3}{5}, \frac{7}{10}$

2 Open

3 a $\frac{1}{10}$ of 50 = **5**
$\frac{2}{10}$ of 50 = **10**
$\frac{7}{10}$ of 50 = **35**

b $\frac{1}{10}$ of 20 = **2**
$\frac{3}{10}$ of 20 = **6**
$\frac{9}{10}$ of 20 = **18**

c $\frac{1}{10}$ of 40 = **4**
$\frac{3}{10}$ of 40 = **12**
$\frac{5}{10}$ of 40 = **20**

Week 10, Lesson 5 – Page 50

Refresher

1 a 2 **b** 4 **c** 3
d 2 **e** 5 **f** 3

2 a $\frac{1}{4}$ **b** $\frac{1}{3}$
c $\frac{3}{4}$ **d** $\frac{1}{4}$

Practice

1 a 8 **b** $\frac{1}{2}$ full **c** $2\frac{1}{2}$ **d** $\frac{1}{4}$
e 1 **f** $\frac{1}{3}$ **g** Open **h** $1\frac{1}{3}$
i $\frac{1}{3}$ **j** 10

Week 11, Lesson 1 – Page 51

Refresher

1 9 − 0 = 9 9 − 1 = 8
9 − 2 = **7** 9 − 3 = **6**
9 − **4** = 5 9 − 5 = 4
9 − 6 = 3 9 − **7** = 2
9 − 8 = **1** 9 − 9 = **0**

2 7 − 4 = 3 7 − 5 = 2
7 − 6 = 1 7 − 7 = 0

Practice

1 16 − 0 = 16 16 − 1 = 15 16 − 2 = 14
16 − 3 = 13 16 − 4 = 12 16 − 5 = 11
16 − 6 = 10 16 − 7 = 9 16 − 8 = 8
16 − 9 = 7 16 − 10 = 6 16 − 11 = 5
16 − 12 = 4 16 − 13 = 3 16 − 14 = 2
16 − 15 = 1 16 − 16 = 0

14 – 0 = 14 | 14 – 1 = 13 | 14 – 2 = 12
14 – 3 = 11 | 14 – 4 = 10 | 14 – 5 = 9
14 – 6 = 8 | 14 – 7 = 7 | 14 – 8 = 6
14 – 9 = 5 | 14 – 10 = 4 | 14 – 11 = 3
14 – 12 = 2 | 14 – 13 = 1 | 14 – 14 = 0

2 19 – 0 = 19 | 19 – 1 = 18 | 19 – 2 = 17
19 – 19 = 0 | 19 – 18 = 1 | 19 – 17 = 2

19 – 3 = 16 | 19 – 4 = 15 | 19 – 5 = 14
19 – 16 = 3 | 19 – 15 = 4 | 19 – 14 = 5

19 – 6 = 13 | 19 – 7 = 12 | 19 – 8 = 11
19 – 13 = 6 | 19 – 12 = 7 | 19 – 11 = 8

19 – 9 = 10
19 – 10 = 9

17 – 1 = 16 | 17 – 2 = 15 | 17 – 3 = 14
17 – 16 = 1 | 17 – 15 = 2 | 17 – 14 = 3

17 – 4 = 13 | 17 – 5 = 12 | 17 – 6 = 11
17 – 13 = 4 | 17 – 12 = 5 | 17 – 11 = 6

17 – 7 = 10 | 17 – 8 = 9
17 – 10 = 7 | 17 – 9 = 8

Week 11, Lesson 2 – Page 52

Refresher

1 a 12 + 5 = 17 | 12 – 5 = 7
5 + 12 = 17 | 12 – 7 = 5
b 7 + 4 = 11 | 7 – 4 = 3
4 + 7 = 11 | 7 – 3 = 4
c 5 + 10 = 15 | 10 – 5 = 5
10 + 5 = 15 | 10 – 5 = 5
d 8 + 13 = 21 | 13 – 8 = 5
13 + 8 = 21 | 13 – 5 = 8
e 9 + 14 = 23 | 14 – 9 = 5
14 + 9 = 23 | 14 – 5 = 9
f 20 + 2 = 22 | 20 – 2 = 18
2 + 20 = 22 | 20 – 18 = 2
g 17 + 8 = 25 | 17 – 8 = 9
8 + 17 = 25 | 17 – 9 = 8
h 19 + 12 = 31 | 19 – 12 = 7
12 + 19 = 31 | 19 – 7 = 12
i 18 + 16 = 34 | 18 – 16 = 2
16 + 18 = 34 | 18 – 2 = 16
j 20 + 11 = 31 | 20 – 11 = 9
11 + 20 = 31 | 20 – 9 = 11

Practice

1 a 18 + 13 = 31 | 13 + 18 = 31
18 – 13 = 5 | 18 – 5 = 13
b 23 + 14 = 37 | 14 + 23 = 37
23 – 14 = 9 | 23 – 9 = 14
c 27 + 21 = 48 | 21 + 27 = 48
27 – 21 = 6 | 27 – 6 = 21
d 46 + 15 = 61 | 15 + 46 = 61
46 – 15 = 31 | 46 – 31 = 15
e 55 + 21 = 76 | 21 + 55 = 76
55 – 21 = 34 | 55 – 34 = 21
f 30 + 67 = 97 | 67 + 30 = 97
67 – 30 = 37 | 67 – 37 = 30
g 29 + 57 = 86 | 57 + 29 = 86
57 – 29 = 28 | 57 – 28 = 29
h 65 + 44 = 109 | 44 + 65 = 109
65 – 44 = 21 | 65 – 21 = 44
i 42 + 86 = 128 | 86 + 42 = 128
86 – 42 = 44 | 86 – 44 = 42
j 94 + 57 = 151 | 51 + 94 = 151
94 – 57 = 37 | 94 – 37 = 57

Week 11, Lesson 3 – Page 53

Refresher

1 a 102 – 98 = **4** | **b** 104 – 97 = **7**
c 106 – 98 = **8** | **d** 101 – 95 = **6**
d 103 – 97 = **6** | **f** 105 – 95 = **10**

Practice

1 a 303 – 298 = **5** | **b** 104 – 99 = **5**
c 103 – 95 = **8** | **d** 101 – 93 = **8**
e 202 – 198 = **4** | **f** 207 – 199 = **8**
g 205 – 199 = **6** | **h** 301 – 297 = **4**
i 404 – 397 = **7** | **j** 502 – 199 = **303**

Week 11, Lesson 4 – Page 54

Refresher

1 a Minutes
b Minutes
c Seconds
d Hours and minutes

Practice

Open

Week 11, Lesson 5 – Page 55

Refresher

1 year is the same as **365** days
1 year is the same as **52** weeks
1 year is the same as **12** months
1 week is the same as **7** days
1 day is the same as **24** hours
1 hour is the same as **60** minutes

Practice

1 He stayed in the water for 15 minutes
2 He arrived at the top at 1:50
3 He slept for 35 minutes
4 He left Sherwood Forest at 9:15
5 She must start at 11:50

Week 12, Lesson 1 – Pages 56 & 57

Refresher

1

Kind of ice	Number
Ice lolly	5
Ice-cream cone	7
Choc-ice	4
Ice-cream tub	6

2 a 6 **b** 5
c Ice-cream cone
d Choc-ice **e** 3

Practice

1 toffee 4 strawberry 9 vanilla 3
chocolate 5 mint 2

2 a 5 **b** strawberry **c** 7
d 6 **e** mint **f** 14

Week 12, Lesson 2 – Pages 58 & 59

Refresher

1

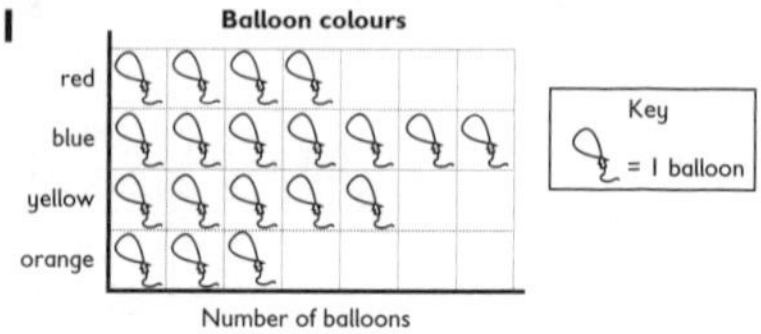

2 a 4 **b** 7 **c** 5
d blue **e** orange **f** 19

Practice

1

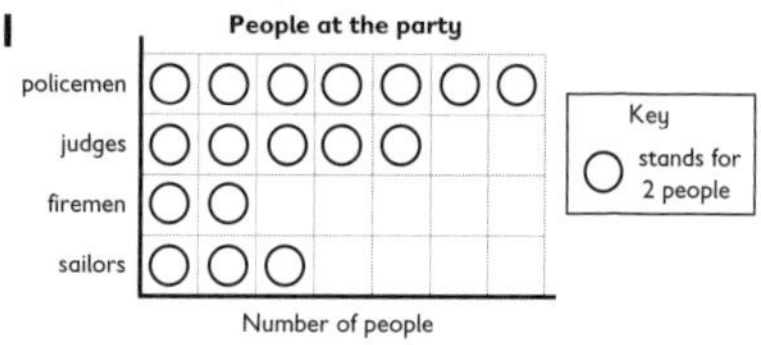

2 a 10 **b** 14 **c** policeman
d 8 **e** 30 **f** 34

Week 12, Lesson 3 – Pages 60 & 61

Refresher

1

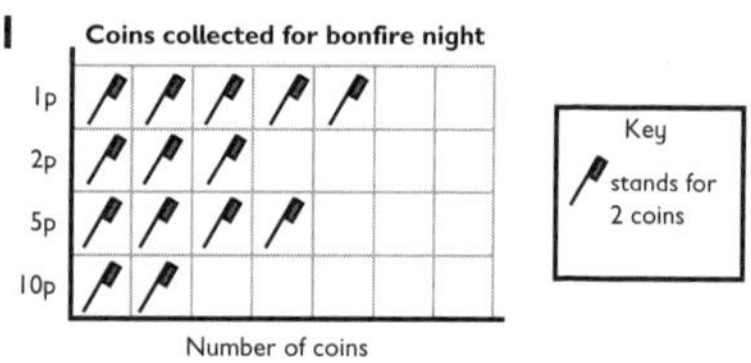

2 a 6 **b** 8 **c** 1p
d 10p **e** 28

Practice

1

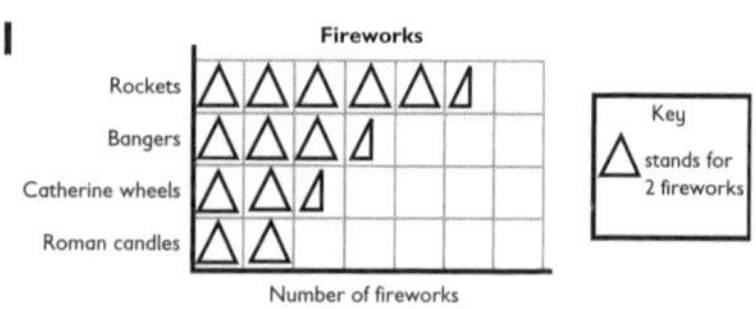

2 a 11 **b** 7 **c** rocket
d 6 **e** 27 **f** 23

Week 12, Lesson 4 – Pages 62 & 63

Refresher

1 a 6 **b** 12 **c** 10

d Bugs

2

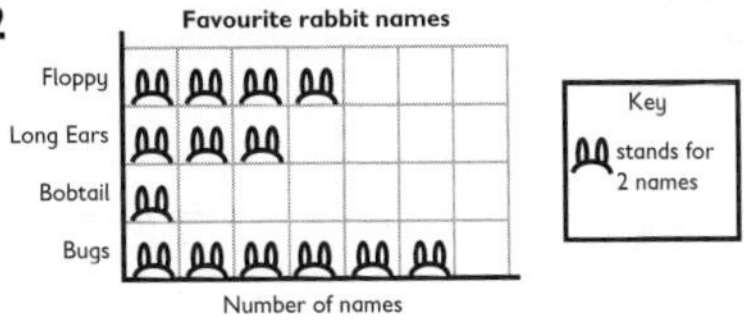

3 a Bobtail **b** 10 **c** 28

Practice

1 a 5 **b** 7

c 30 **d** Lassie

2

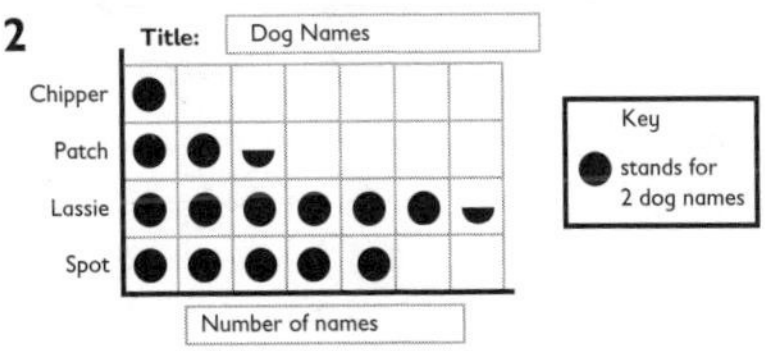

3 a Chipper. Least pictures

b 8

c 20

Week 12, Lesson 5 – Page 64

Refresher

1

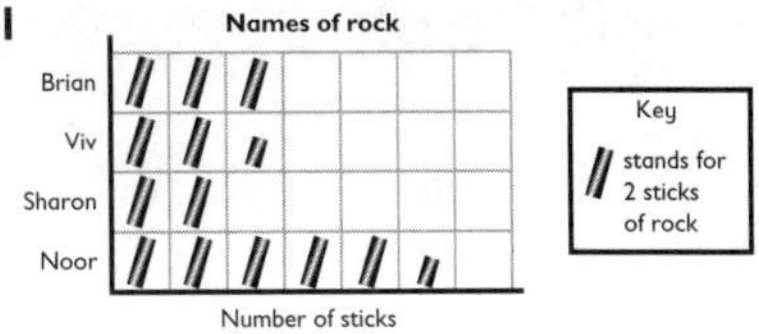

2 a Noor **b** 6 **c** 5

d 4 **e** 11

Practice

1 Open (answers will vary)

2 Open (answers will vary)

3 Open (answers will vary)

Answers

Pupil Book 2

Spring

Week 1, Lesson 1 – Page 5

Refresher

1 a 3rd **banana** b 1st **pear**
c ninth **banana** d 7th **apple**
e tenth **pear** f 13th **banana**
g twentieth **banana**
h 18th **banana**

2 first, 1st; fifth, 5th; eighth, 8th; tenth, 10th; twelfth, 12th; seventeenth; 17th

Practice

Open

Week 1, Lesson 2 – Page 6

Refresher

a 30 m b 40 m c 40 m
d 50 m e 50 m f 50 m

Practice

1 a 20 m b 90 m c 50 m
d 20 m e 10 m

2 a 40 m b 50 m c 20 m
d 100 m e 10 m

Week 1, Lesson 3 – Page 7

Refresher

1 a 5 kg b 700 g
c 75 g d 15 g

2 a about 3 kg b about 400 g
c about 20 g d about 10 g

Practice

1 a 11 kg b 700 g
c 350 g d 25 g

2 a about 4 kg b about 100 g
c about 300 g d about 45 g

Week 2, Lesson 1 – Page 8

Refresher

Answers will vary

Practice

Answers will vary

Week 2, Lesson 2 – Page 9

Refresher

Open

Practice

Open

Week 2, Lesson 3 – Page 10

Refresher

1 a 6+5+3=**14** b 4+7+2=**13**
c 9+3+4=**16** d 5+3+6=**14**
e 7+2+1=**10** f 4+6+3=**13**
g 6+3+7=**16** h 5+4+7=**16**
i 5+2+6=**13** j 1+6+4=**11**

Practice

1 a 6+3+4+5=**18** b 9+2+5+1=**17**
c 7+4+6+5=**22** d 8+3+6+2=**19**
e 9+7+5+1=**22** f 6+9+7+3=**25**
g 4+5+8+7=**24** h 6+8+7+2=**23**
i 9+5+4+6=**24** j 9+8+7+6=**30**

Week 2, Lesson 4 – Page 11

Refresher

a 11+7+3=21 b 5+5+8=18
c 8+2+4=14 d 9+1+7=17
e 6+4+8=18 f 7+3+9=19
g 1+9+12=22 h 5+5+9=19
i 4+6+7=17

Practice

1 a 6+4+16=26 b 2+8+19=29
c 3+7+18=28 d 4+5+14=23
e 5+6+17=28 f 7+2+6=15
g 6+15+2+3=26 h 2+5+7+19=33
i 2+12+3+9=26

Week 2, Lesson 5 – Page 12

Refresher

1 a 15+5+3 **b** 15+5+2 **c** 15+5+4
d 25+5+1 **e** 25+5+3 **f** 25+5+2
g 35+5+4 **h** 35+5+1 **i** 35+5+3

Practice

1 a 25+2+5+4 **b** 25+3+5+2
c 25+1+5+3 **d** 35+4+5+1
e 45+1+5+4 **f** 45+2+5+3
g 55+3+5+4 **h** 45+3+5+2
i 55+2+5+1 **j** 65+1+5+3
k 65+3+5+3 **l** 75+4+5+2
m 15+1+25+2 **n** 25+1+15+3
o 15+4+35+1

Week 3, Lesson 1 – Page 13

Refresher

1 100, 200, 300, 400, 500, 600, 700, 800, 900, 1000

2 a 700 **b** 400 **c** 600 **d** 200
e 1000 **f** 100 **g** 300 **h** 800

3 a 600 **b** 800 **c** 300 **d** 100
e 900 **f** 200 **g** 700 **h** 500

Practice

1 a **200** + 800 = 1000 2+8
b 400 + **600** = 1000 4+6
c 900 + **100** = 1000 9+1
d 500 + **500** = 1000 5+5
e 700 + **300** = 1000 7+3
f **0** + 1000 = 1000 0+10
g **600** + 400 = 1000 6+4
h 100 + **900** = 1000 1+9
i 200 + **800** = 1000 2+8
j **700** + 300 = 1000 7+3

Week 3, Lesson 2 – Page 14

Refresher

1 5, 10, 15, 20, 25, 30, 35, 40, 45, 50, 55, 60, 65, 70, 75, 80, 85, 90, 95, 100

2 a 55 **b** 85 **c** 35
d 65 **e** 15

3 a 25 **b** 65 **c** 35
d 95 **e** 45

4 a 80 **b** 50 **c** 30
d 10 **e** 60 **f** 80

Practice

1 a 95+**5**=100 **b** 45+**55**=100
90+10 40+50
100+0 50+50
c **25**+75=100 **d** 85+**15**=100
20+80 80+20
30+70 90+10
e 65+**35**=100 **f** 5+**95**=100
60+40 10+90
70+30 0+100
g **75**+25=100 **h** **85**+15=100
70+30 90+10
80+20 80+20
i **45**+55=100
40+50
50+40

Week 3, Lesson 3 – Page 15

Refresher

Open

Practice

Open

Week 3, Lesson 4 – Page 16

Refresher

1 20 **2** 3
3 3 **4** 40

Practice

1 44 **2** 6
3 12 **4** 18, 10

Week 3, Lesson 5 – Page 17

Refresher

1 55p **2** 85p
3 20p **4** 50p

Practice

1 £1 **2** £2.25
3 65p **4** £1, £1, 50p

Week 4, Lesson 1 – Page 18

Refresher

Open

Practice

Open

Week 4, Lesson 2 – Page 19

Refresher

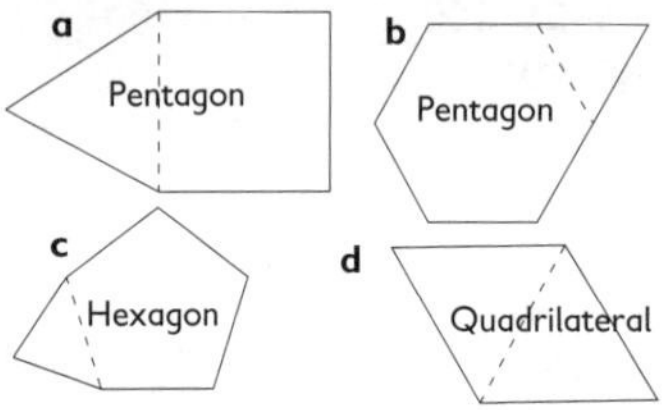

Practice

1

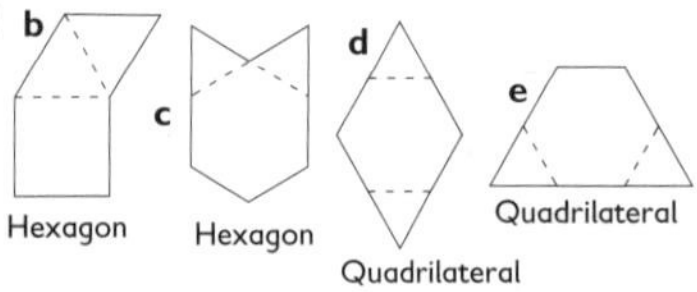

2

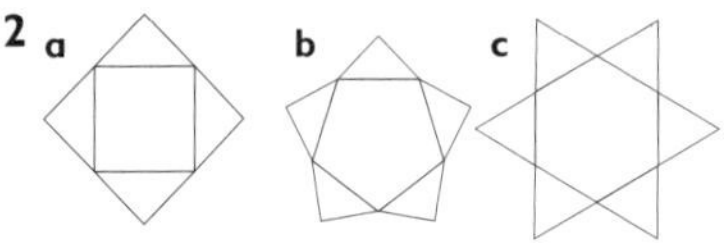

Week 4, Lesson 3 – Page 20

Refresher

1

R	B	B	Y	Y
Y	Y	R	R	B
B	R	Y	B	R

Practice

1 a 6 ways – ie.

B	B	R	R	Y	Y
RY	YR	BY	YB	BR	RB

b 6 ways – ie.

RY	YR	BY	YB	BR	RB
B	B	R	R	Y	Y

Week 4, Lesson 4 – Page 21

Refresher

Open

Practice

Open

Week 4, Lesson 5 – Page 22

Refresher

1 Beta — **2** Delta

3 North — **4** West

Practice

1 a North — **b** Delta

2 a East — **b** Make a quarter turn to the left. Fly North.

3 a On the supply ship — **b** West

4 a West — **b** Beta Rig

Week 5, Lesson 1 – Page 23

Refresher

1 a silver mine — **b** High Peak Pass

c Reservation — **d** Double D Ranch

Practice

Open

Week 5, Lesson 2 – Page 24

Refresher

Open

Practice

1 a

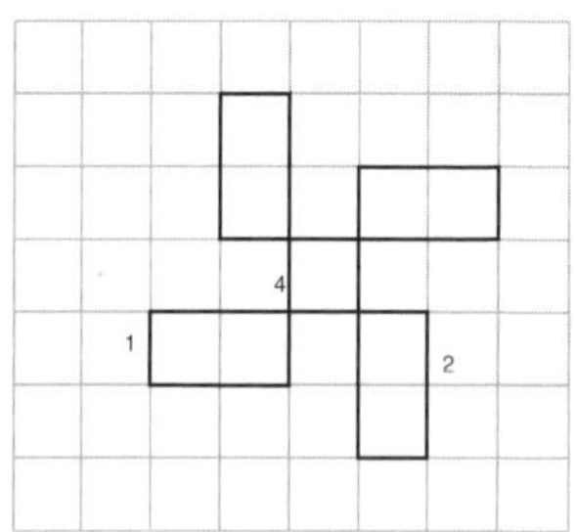

b

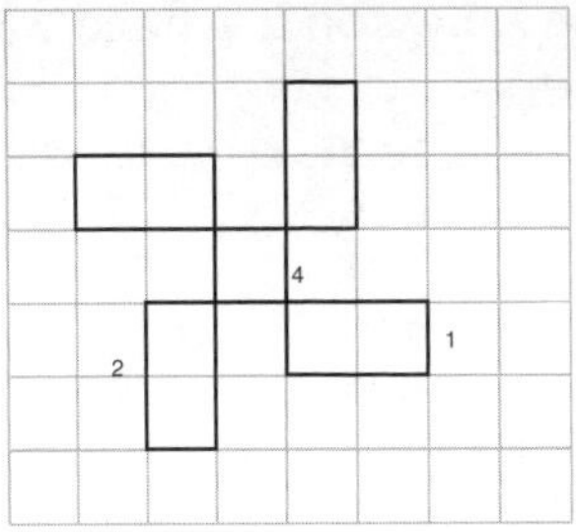

2 & **3** – Open

Week 5, Lesson 3 – Page 25

Refresher

1 a 3:00, 3:05, 3:10, **3:15**, **3:20**, **3:25**, 3:30.
b 4:25, 4:30, 4:35, **4:40**, **4:45**, **4:50**, **4:55**.
c 8:45, 8:50, **8:55**, **9:00**, **9:05**, **9:10**, **9:15**.
2 a 7:25 **b** 1:45 **c** 9:10

Practice

1 a 40 minutes past 7
20 minutes to 8
b 55 minutes past 9
5 minutes to 10
c 35 minutes past 1
25 minutes to 2
d 50 minutes past 6
10 minutes to 7
e 45 minutes past 12
15 minutes to 1
2 a 3:35 **b** 3:55
c 3:25 **d** 4:05
3 9:05 a.m., 10:00 a.m., 11:40 a.m., 12:35 p.m., 1:50 p.m., 4:25 p.m.

Week 5, Lesson 4 – Page 26

Refresher

1 a = < 3kg **b** = > 4kg
c = < 3kg **d** = < 7kg

Practice

1 a $\frac{1}{2}$ kg **b** 1000g **c** 5kg
d $1\frac{1}{2}$ kg **e** 500g **f** $2\frac{1}{2}$ kg
2 a B **b** C **c** D
d F **e** A **f** C

Week 5, Lesson 5 – Page 27

Refresher

1 Kevin 1 (200 g)
Kitty (open – 0×200 g + 5×100 g etc.)

Practice

1

Child	500 g	200 g	100 g
Abby	1	2	1
Bert	1	2	3
Cindy	0	4	2
Dan	0	2	6
Eli	2	0	0
Fran	0	5	0
Jill	1	0	5
Hetty	0	3	4
Iyaz	0	1	8
Jenny	0	0	10

2 Answers will vary

Week 6, Lesson 1 – Page 28

Refresher

1 a 3 large eggs 100 g bacon
50 g mushrooms 25 g butter
b 12 large eggs 400 g bacon
200 g mushrooms 100 g butter

Practice

1 a 200 g pasta
150 g mussels
100 g prawns
250 g plum tomatoes
10 g chilli pepper
50 g Parmesan cheese
1 clove garlic
b 400 g rice noodles
250 g cooked chicken
100 g prawns
200 g beansprouts
60 g onion
120 g cooking oil

Answer to chef's question – **100 g**

Week 6, Lesson 2 – Page 29

Refresher

1 (At 2 months)
Daisy weighs 5 kg and 500 g, or $5\frac{1}{2}$ kg.
Dixie weighs 6 kg and 500 g, or $6\frac{1}{2}$ kg.
Dolly weighs 4 kg and 500 g, or $4\frac{1}{2}$ kg.

2 (At 4 months)
Daisy weighs 12 kg and 500 g, or $12\frac{1}{2}$ kg.
Dixie weighs 12 kg and 0 g, or 12 kg.
Dolly weighs 11 kg and 500 g, or $11\frac{1}{2}$ kg.

Practice

1 a Dixie **b** Dolly **c** Daisy

2 Daisy 11 kg 300 g
Dixie 11 kg 100 g
Dolly 12 kg 0 g

Week 6, Lesson 3 – Page 30

Refresher

1 a 3 kg **b** 30 g **c** 5 kg
d 25 kg **e** 700 kg **f** 6000 kg

Practice

1 a 300 g **b** 2400 g
c 90 g **d** 60 g

2 a 1000 g / 1 kg **b** 2000 g / 2 kg
c 2500 g / 2.5 kg

Week 7, Lesson 1 – Page 31

Refresher

1 3, 6, 9, 12, **15**, **18**, **21**, **24**, **27**, 30

2a 15 **b** 21 **c** 9
d 27 **e** 12 **f** 33

3a 3 **b** 27 **c** 12
d 24 **e** 6 **f** 30

Practice

1

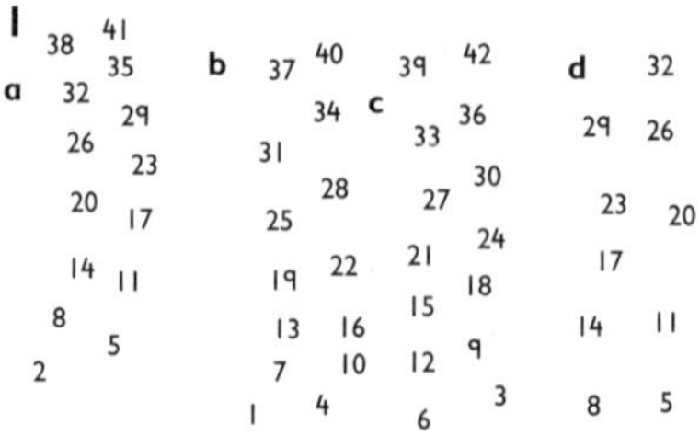

Week 7, Lesson 2 – Page 32

Refresher

1 4, 8, 12, 16, 20, 24, 28, 32, 36, 40

2a 12 **b** 20 **c** 28
d 44 **e** 36 **f** 8

3a 16 **b** 4 **c** 12
d 32 **e** 36 **f** 20

Practice

1 a 7, 11, **15**, **19**, **23**
b **14**, **18**, **22**, **26**, **30**
c **21**, **25**, **29**, **33**, **37**
d **28**, **32**, **36**, **40**, **44**

Week 7, Lesson 3 – Page 33

Refresher

1 a 2, 6, **10**, **14**, 18, **22**, **26**, 30
b 3, 8, 13, **18**, **23**, **28**, **33**, **38**
c 1, 4, **7**, **10**, **13**, **16**, 19, **22**
d 50, 45, 40, **35**, **30**, **25**, **20**
e 40, 36, **32**, **28**, **24**, **20**, **16**

Practice

1 Three cards missing – **9** and **33** (in multiples of 3 circle) **24** (in the middle)

2

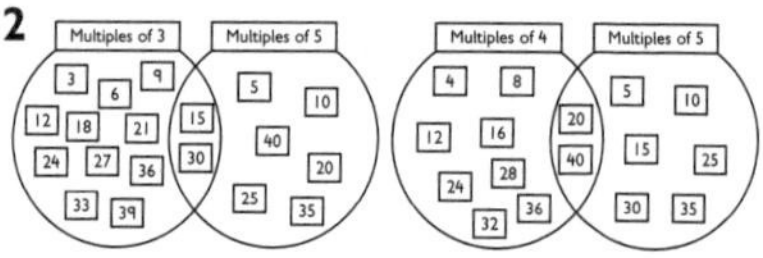

Week 7, Lesson 4 – Page 34

Refresher

Open

Practice

1 The numbers all add up to 3, 6 or 9 (multiples of 3)

2 The numbers 2, 5 and 8 repeat themselves

Week 7, Lesson 5 – Page 35

Refresher

Open

Practice

Open

Week 8, Lesson 1 – Page 36

Refresher

1 a 38 b 37 c 36
d 49 e 58 f 69
g 78 h 69

Practice

1 a 122 b 63 c 97
d 98 e 123 f 182
g 150 h 142

Week 8, Lesson 2 – Page 37

Refresher

1 a 40 b 59 c 57
d 69 e 99 f 98
g 109 h 119

Practice

1 a 90 b 102 c 176
d 223 e 89 f 163
g 136 h 198

Week 8, Lesson 3 – Page 38

Refresher

a 12+15+31=58 12+15+42=69
12+31+42=85 15+31+42=88
b 34+14+43=91 34+14+21=69
34+43+21=98 14+43+21=78
c 52+11+35=98 52+35+23=110
52+11+23=86 11+35+23=69

Practice

a 36+22+57+45=160
36+22+57+61=176
36+22+45+61=164
36+57+45+61=199
22+57+45+61=185

b 82+17+29+38=166
82+17+29+53=181
82+17+38+53=190
82+29+38+53=202
17+29+38+53–137

c 52+87+34+27=200
52+87+34+98=271
52+87+27+98=264
52+34+27+98=211
87+34+27+98=246

Week 8, Lesson 4 – Page 39

Refresher

1 23 2 10
3 5 4 16

Practice

1 8 2 36
3 4 4 64

Week 8, Lesson 5 – Page 40

Refresher

1 a 20÷2=10 b 15÷3=5 c 16÷4=4
d 12÷3=4 e 14÷2=7 f 20÷4=5

Practice

1 b 4×7=28 7×4=28
28÷4=7 28÷7=4
c 3×6=18 6×3=18
18÷3=6 18÷6=3
d 5×2=10 2×5=10
10÷2=5 10÷5=2
e 3×7=21 7×3=21
21÷3=7 21÷7=3
f 4×2=8 2×4=8
8÷4=2 8÷2=4

Week 9, Lesson 1 – Page 41

Refresher

1 a 6×2=12 3×2=6
7×2=14 4×2=8
b 8×5=40 9×5=45
4×5=20 7×5=35
c 9×10=90 8×10=80
3×10=30 6×10=60
7×10=70

Practice

1 a 4×2=8 2×4=8
8÷2=4 8÷4=2
b 6×5=30 5×6=30
30÷5=6 30÷6=5

c 4×9 = 36   9×4 = 36
36÷9 = 4   36÷4 = 9
d 5×7=35   7×5=35
35÷7=5   35÷5=7
e 2×8=16   8×2=16
16÷2=8   16÷8=2
f 3×10=30   10×3=30
30÷10=3   30÷3=10

2 a 6×2=12   2×6=12
12÷2=6   12÷6=2
b 8×10=80   10×8=80
80÷10=8   80÷8=10
c 7×5=35   5×7=35
35÷5=7   35÷7=5
d 9×5=45   5×9=45
45÷9=5   45÷5=9

Week 9, Lesson 2 – Page 42

Refresher

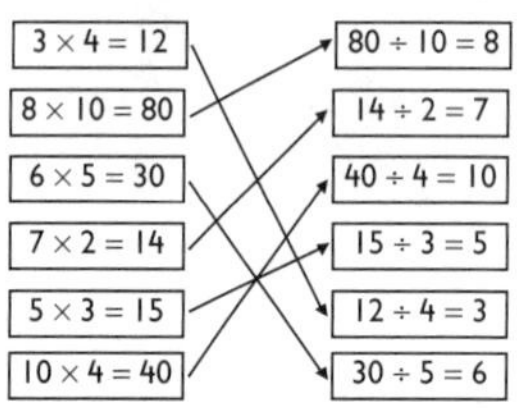

Practice

1 a 25÷5=5   5 roses each
b 12÷3=4   £4 each
c 80÷10=8   8 classes
d 21÷7=3   3 vases
e 35÷5=7   7 bunches
f 20÷10=2   £2 for 1 daisy

Week 9, Lesson 3 – Page 43

Refresher

1 a 20÷5=**4**   30÷10=**3**
12÷2=**6**   35÷5=**7**
b 16÷4=**4**   9÷3=**3**
4÷2=**2**   25÷5=**5**
c 100÷10=**10**   40÷5=**8**
18÷2=**9**   12÷3=**4**

Practice

1 a 45÷9=9 **9 chocolate bars**
b 24÷4=6 **6 cakes in each bag**
c 27÷3=9 **9p each**
d 16÷8=2 **2 doughnuts each**

2 a 20+25=45   45÷5=9
It will take 9 weeks
b 15+13=28   28÷7=4
They use 4 pages

3 a 15÷5=3   8÷4=2
20÷4=5   3+2+5=10
She spends £10
b 8×5=40   9×3=27   40−27=13
It costs £13 more

Week 9, Lesson 4 – Page 44

Refresher

1 Double each number
34 10 100 600
300 40 160

2 Halve each number
50 10 25 12
8 40 200

Practice

1 a 11 14
17 32 25
b 45 70 85
55 40
c 350 500 300
450 250
d 170 130 90
70
e 26 36 32
22
f 500 700 300
900

Week 9, Lesson 5 – Page 45

Refresher

(16)	16+16=32	32+32=**64**
(15)	15+15=30	30+30=**60**
(30)	30+30=60	60+60=**120**
(12)	12+12=24	24+24=**48**
(7)	7+7=14	14+14=**28**
(10)	10+10=20	20+20=**40**
(8)	8+8=16	16+16=**32**
(18)	18+18=36	36+36=**72**
(25)	25+25=50	50+50 = **100**
(19)	9+9=18	18+18 = **36**

Practice

1 a $4\times2=8$ $4\times4=16$
b $8\times2=16$ $8\times4=32$
c $6\times2=12$ $6\times4=24$
d $3\times2=6$ $3\times4=12$
e $9\times2=18$ $9\times4=36$
f $7\times2=14$ $7\times4=28$
g $5\times2=10$ $5\times4=20$
h $10\times2=20$ $10\times4=40$

Week 10, Lesson 1 – Pages 46 & 47

Refresher

1 a quarter $\frac{1}{4}$ b third $\frac{1}{3}$ c fifth $\frac{1}{5}$
d tenth $\frac{1}{10}$ e half $\frac{1}{2}$

Practice

1 a quarter $\frac{1}{4}$ b third $\frac{1}{3}$ c tenth $\frac{1}{10}$
d half $\frac{1}{2}$ e fifth $\frac{1}{5}$
2 b 5 c 16 d 20 e 16
f 15 g 9 h 24

Week 10, Lesson 2 – Pages 48 & 49

Refresher

1 Answers will vary
2 Ben gets 6 biscuits
Amir gets 3 biscuits
Emma gets 3 biscuits

Practice

1 a $(\frac{1}{2})$ + e $(\frac{1}{2})$ = whole cake
l $(\frac{1}{4})$ + o $(\frac{1}{4})$ + b $(\frac{1}{2})$ = whole cake
i $(\frac{1}{4})$ + k $(\frac{1}{4})$ + d $(\frac{1}{4})$ + g $(\frac{1}{4})$ = whole cake
j $(\frac{1}{4})$ + c $(\frac{1}{4})$ + n $(\frac{1}{2})$ = whole cake
h $(\frac{1}{2})$ + f $(\frac{1}{4})$ + m $(\frac{1}{4})$ = whole cake
2 Gurjit gets **10** biscuits
Zoe gets **5** biscuits
Ann gets **5** biscuits

Week 10, Lesson 3 – Pages 50 & 51

Refresher

1 a $\frac{1}{4}$ b $\frac{1}{3}$
c $\frac{1}{6}$ d $\frac{4}{10}$ (or $\frac{2}{5}$)

Practice

1 a $\frac{1}{2}$ b $\frac{1}{5}$
c $\frac{1}{3}$ d $\frac{3}{4}$
e $\frac{3}{5}$ f $\frac{1}{5}$
g $\frac{1}{2}$ h $\frac{2}{5}$
i $\frac{4}{10}$ j $\frac{2}{10}$

Week 10, Lesson 4 – Pages 52 & 53

Refresher

a $\frac{2}{10}$ full $\frac{8}{10}$ empty
b $\frac{4}{10}$ full $\frac{6}{10}$ empty
c $\frac{9}{10}$ full $\frac{1}{10}$ empty
d $\frac{5}{10}$ full $\frac{5}{10}$ empty
e $\frac{3}{10}$ full $\frac{7}{10}$ empty

Practice

1 a and c
2 a Pour out $\frac{2}{10}$ b Add $\frac{2}{10}$
c Add $\frac{4}{10}$ d Pour out $\frac{4}{10}$
e Pour out $\frac{1}{10}$ f Add $\frac{1}{10}$

Week 10, Lesson 5 – Pages 54 & 55

Refresher

a $\frac{1}{2}, \frac{1}{2}$ b $\frac{1}{5}, \frac{4}{5}$ c $\frac{1}{5}, \frac{4}{5}$
d $\frac{1}{4}, \frac{3}{4}$ e $\frac{1}{3}, \frac{2}{3}$

Practice

1 a $\frac{3}{4}$ b $\frac{7}{10}$ c $\frac{1}{2}$
d $\frac{2}{5}$ e $\frac{8}{10}$ f $\frac{5}{10}$
g $\frac{3}{5}$ h $\frac{1}{4}$ i $\frac{3}{10}$
2 a $\frac{1}{4} + \frac{1}{4}$
b $\frac{1}{3} + \frac{1}{3} + \frac{1}{3}$
c $\frac{1}{4} + \frac{1}{4} + \frac{1}{4} + \frac{1}{4}$

Week 11, Lesson 1 – Pages 56 & 57

Refresher

Colour	Number
Red	6
Blue	10
Yellow	7
Black	6
Orange	3

Practice

See table above to check bar charts

1 Blue **2** 4 **3** 22

Week 11, Lesson 2 – Pages 58 & 59

Refresher

1 Red 5 Yellow 3
Blue 8 Orange 1

Practice

1 Cola 8 Lemonade 2
Orange 12 Cherry 6

Week 11, Lesson 3 – Pages 60 & 61

Refresher

	Tally	Total
Bus stops	II	2
Houses	~~IIII~~ ~~IIII~~ I	11
Cars	~~IIII~~ III	8
Zebra crossings	II	2
People	~~IIII~~ ~~IIII~~ I	11

Practice

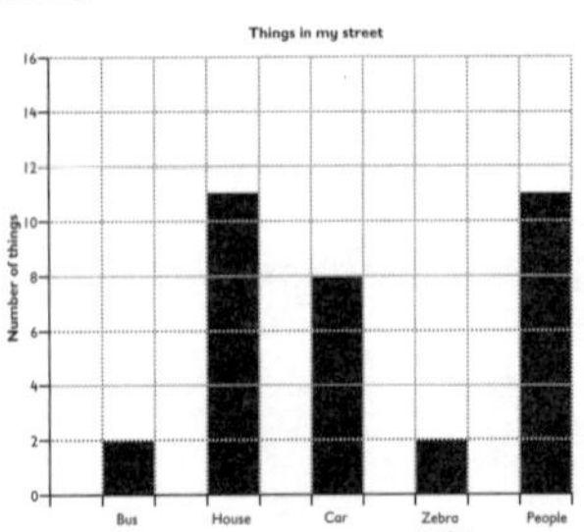

1 a houses and people **b** houses **c** 10

Week 11, Lesson 4 – Pages 62 & 63

Refresher

Bananas	People
3	5
4	6
5	4
6	3
7	1

Practice

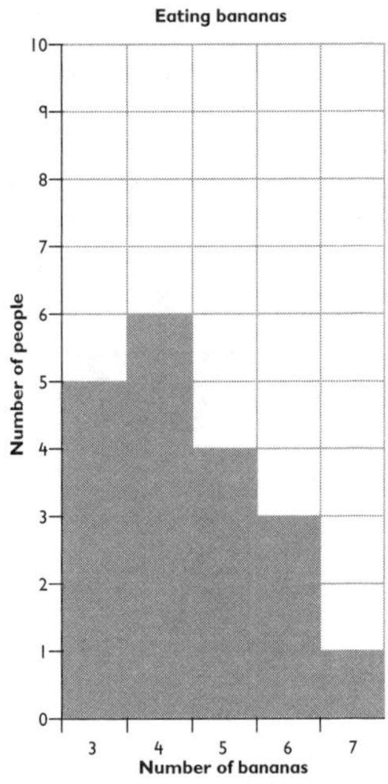

1 a 7 bananas **b** 7 people
c 5 people

Week 11, Lesson 5 – Page 64 & 65

Refresher

Open – answers will vary

Practice

Answers will vary

Answers

Pupil Book 3

Summer

Week 1, Lesson 1 – Page 5

Refresher

1 a £500 **b** £650 **c** £150

2 Open

3 261, 262, 263, 265, 268, 269

Practice

1 a 145 **b** 352 **c** 352

2 a Numbers 201 to 299 are in the hat

b Numbers 176 to 209 are in the hat

c Numbers 85 to 109 are in the hat

d Numbers 350 to 393 are in the hat

3 93, 108, 200, 235, 512, 629, 951

Week 1, Lesson 2 – Page 6

Refresher

a 600 g **b** 500 g **c** 700 g

Practice

1 a 200 g **b** 800 g **c** 100 g

d 400 g **e** 0 g

2 a 200 kg **b** 800 kg **c** 100 kg

d 400 kg **e** 100 kg

3 Answers will vary

Week 1, Lesson 3 – Page 7

Refresher

a 7 **b** 1 **c** $8\frac{1}{2}$

d 3 **e** 900 **f** 400

g 700 **h** 40 **i** 85

j 10

Practice

a 3 **b** $9\frac{1}{2}$ **c** 2

d 5 **e** 600 **f** 850

g 450 **h** 65 **I** 30

j 50

Week 2, Lesson 1 – Page 8

Refresher

1 a 48 **b** 72 **c** 96

d 83 **e** 65 **f** 82

g 128 **h** 154 **i** 232

j 162 **k** 247 **l** 229

Practice

1 a 126+10+1=**137** **b** 262+10+1=**273**

c 319+10−1=**328** **d** 194+10−1=**203**

e 283−10−1=**272** **f** 327−10−1=**316**

g 653−10+1=**644** **h** 439−10+1=**430**

i 521+10−1=**530** **j** 752−10−1=**741**

k 845+10+1=**856** **l** 971−10+1=**962**

Week 2, Lesson 2 – Page 9

Refresher

Answers will vary

Practice

Answers will vary

Week 2, Lesson 3 – Page 10

Refresher

1 a 6 16 26 66 96

b 6 26 46 76 386

c 67 177 147 257 237

d 1 11 31 61 111

e 7 27 37 57 77

f 69 129 159 179 229

Practice

1 a 136 166 276 336 466

b 174 514 264 784 354

c 162 232 312 472 922

d 248 818 628 758 198

e 289 569 929 459 669

f 494 594 294 794 94

Week 2, Lesson 4 – Page 11

Answers will vary

Week 2, Lesson 5 – Page 12

Refresher

1 a 131 **b** 142 **c** 154
d 163 **e** 175 **f** 149
g 158 **h** 187 **i** 192

2 a 59 **b** 56 **c** 38
d 77 **e** 48 **f** 38
g 58 **h** 78 **i** 68

Practice

1 a 267 **b** 254 **c** 348
d 887 **e** 621 **f** 963
g 572 **h** 784 **i** 812

2 a 94 **b** 89 **c** 88
d 96 **e** 97 **f** 79
g 79 **h** 86 **i** 97

Week 3, Lesson 1 – Page 13

Refresher

1 a 6 16 26 36
b 8 18 28 38
c 7 17 27 37
d 33 23 13
e 31 21
f 6 60 600

Practice

1 a 72 62 52
42 22 12
b 19 29 39
49 79 99
c 17 27 37
47 67 87
d 94 84 74
64 54 44
e 84 74 64
54 24 14
f 15 150 1500

Week 3, Lesson 2 – Page 14

Refresher

1 a 48 **b** 56 **c** 48
d 68 **e** 59 **f** 97
g 92 **h** 92 **i** 91
j 81 **k** 85 **l** 110
m 119 **n** 157 **o** 126
p 112 **q** 127 **r** 142

Practice

1 a 132 **b** 133 **c** 159
d 176 **e** 194 **f** 178
g 175 **h** 174 **i** 185
j 202 **k** 200 **l** 186
m 237 **n** 238 **o** 241
p 232 **q** 245 **r** 243

Week 3, Lesson 3 – Page 15

Refresher

a 57 **b** 59 **c** 68
d 69 **e** 88 **f** 102
g 81 **h** 83 **i** 94
j 91

Practice

a 159 **b** 179 **c** 197
d 175 **e** 196 **f** 194
g 225 **h** 219 **i** 235
j 221

Week 3, Lesson 4 – Page 16

Refresher

1 91p 40+51=91p
2 49p £1.00−51p=49p
3 60p £1.00−40p=60p
4 £1.71 £1.20+51p=£1.71
5 80p £2.00−£1.20=80p

Practice

1 a £2.11 51p+40p+£1.20=£2.11
b £2.89 £5.00-£2.11=£2.89
2 £1 40p+40p+20p=£1
3 £2.09 £5.00−£1.20−£1.20−51p=£2.09
4 £3.09 £1.49+£2.00−40p=£3.09
5 £4.22 40p+40p+51p+51p+£1.20+£1.20=£4.22

Week 3, Lesson 5 – Page 17

Refresher

1 21 + 9 = **30** 2 40 + 14 = **54**
3 16 − 9 = **7** 4 14 + 14 = **28**
5 21 − 6 = **15**

Practice

1 14 + 21 + 16 + 40 + 9 = **100**
2 100 − 9 = **91**
3 100 − 16 − 14 = **70**
4 100 − 21 − 40 = **39**
5 100 + 21 = **121**

Week 4, Lesson 1 – Page 18

Refresher

a $\frac{1}{2}$ litre **b** 2 litres **c** $4\frac{1}{2}$ litres
d 4 litres **e** 1 litre **f** $2\frac{1}{2}$ litres
g $3\frac{1}{2}$ litres **h** 3 litres

Practice

1 a This jug holds $\frac{1}{2}$ litre or 500 ml of orange juice.
b This jug holds 2 litres or 2000 ml of orange juice.
c This jug holds $4\frac{1}{2}$ litres or 4500 ml of orange juice.
d This jug holds 4 litres or 4000 ml of orange juice.
e This jug holds 1 litre or 1000 ml of orange juice.
f This jug holds $2\frac{1}{2}$ litres or 2500 ml of orange juice.
g This jug holds $3\frac{1}{2}$ litres or 3500 ml of orange juice.
h This jug holds 3 litres or 3000 ml of orange juice.

2 a $4\frac{1}{2}$ litres **b** 3 litres **c** $\frac{1}{2}$ litre
d 1 litre **e** 4 litres **f** $2\frac{1}{2}$ litres
g $1\frac{1}{2}$ litres **h** 2 litres

Week 4, Lesson 2 – Page 19

Open

Week 4, Lesson 3 – Page 20

Refresher

1 a salad dressing, apple juice, tomato sauce, fizzy cola, shampoo
b tomato sauce, shampoo, fizzy cola, salad dressing, apple juice
2 They are in a different order (ie. smaller height doesn't mean smaller capacity)

Practice

1 tomato sauce 300 ml
olive oil 1000 ml
salad dressing 500 ml
orange drink 1500 ml
2 shampoo 1600 ml
shower gel 1200 ml
toothpaste 400 ml

Week 4, Lesson 4 – Page 21

Refresher

a, b, d and e are all true statements

Practice

1 a 1000 ml **b** 500 ml
c 15l **d** 4l
2 a 1l 500 ml ↔ $1\frac{1}{2}$l
2l 500 ml ↔ **$2\frac{1}{2}$l**
5l 500 ml ↔ $5\frac{1}{2}$l
7l 500 ml ↔ **$7\frac{1}{2}$l**
10l 500 ml ↔ $10\frac{1}{2}$l
b 3.5l ↔ 3l 500 ml
4.5l ↔ **4l 500 ml**
6.5l ↔ 6l 500 ml
8.5l ↔ $8\frac{1}{2}$l
9.5l ↔ **$9\frac{1}{2}$l**

Week 4, Lesson 5 – Page 22

Refresher

a 1 spoon holds **5 ml**
b 2 spoons hold **10 ml**
c 4 spoons hold **20 ml**
d 5 spoons hold **25 ml**

e 10 spoons hold **50 ml**
f 20 spoons hold 100 ml

Practice

a 1 spoon every day for 10 days – **50 ml bottle**
b 2 spoons twice a day for 5 days – **100 ml bottle**
c 3 spoons every day for 5 days – **75 ml bottle**
d 1 spoon 3 times a day for 10 days – **150 ml bottle**
e 2 spoons twice a day for 10 days – **200 ml bottle**

2

Spoons	How often per day	Number of days	Amount
1	8	10	400 ml
2	4	10	400 ml
4	2	10	400 ml
8	1	10	400 ml

Week 5, Lesson 1 – Page 23

Refresher

Lines of symmetry	triangle
none	c, d
one	a, f
more than one	b, e

Practice

1 a g **b** b, d, e **c** a, c, f, h
2 Open (ie. using a mirror)

Week 5, Lesson 2 – Page 24

Refresher

Open

Practice

Open

Week 5, Lesson 3 – Page 25

Refresher

Open

Practice

Open

Week 5, Lesson 4 – Page 26

Refresher

Open

Practice

a circle **b** parallelogram
c square **d** square (or triangle)
e hexagon **f** pentagon
g octagon

Week 5, Lesson 5 – Page 27

Refresher

I face the	two $\frac{1}{4}$ turns right	I now face the
pyramid	→	camel
camel	→	pyramid
obelisk	→	tour bus
tour bus	→	obelisk

I face the	I make	I now face the
camel	two $\frac{1}{4}$ turns left	pyramid
obelisk	two $\frac{1}{4}$ turns right	tour bus
pyramid	a $\frac{1}{2}$ turn left	camel
tour bus	a $\frac{1}{2}$ turn right	obelisk

I face the	in the opposite direction	object
pyramid	→	camel
obelisk	→	tour bus
camel	→	pyramid

Practice

3 a obelisk **b** pyramid **c** camel

Week 6, Lesson 1 – Page 28

Refresher

2 Right angles

Less than	More than
b, c	a, d

Practice

3 Right angles

Less than	About right angle	More than
h, b, f	d, g, k, j	a, c,e, i

Week 6, Lesson 2 – Page 29

Refresher

Open

Practice

Open

Week 6, Lesson 3 – Page 30

Refresher

Open

Practice

Open

Week 7, Lesson 1 – Page 31

Refresher

1 a … 58, 60, 62, 64, 66, 68, 70
  b … 110, 112, 114, 116, 118, 120
2 a 75, 80, 85, 90, 95, 100, 105
  b 120, 125, 130, 135, 140, 145, 150
3 a 60, 70, 80, 90, 100, 110, 120
  b 130, 140, 150, 160, 170, 180, 190

Practice

1 a Multiples of 5: odd one out: 332
  b Multiples of 10: odd ones out: 145, 122
   Multiples of 5: odd one out: 122
   Multiples of 2: odd one out: 145
  c Multiples of 10: odd ones out: 225, 273
   Multiples of 5: odd one out: 273
   Multiples of 2: odd ones out: 225, 273
  d Multiples of 5: odd ones out: 202, 793
  e Multiples of 5: odd ones out: 362, 624
  f Multiples of 10: odd ones out: 485, 362
   Multiples of 5: odd one out: 362
   Multiples of 2: odd one out: 485
  g Multiples of 2: odd ones out: 301, 405

Week 7, Lesson 2 – Page 32

Refresher

1 a 100, 200, 300, 400, 500, 600, 700, 800, 900, 1000
  b 50, 100, 150, 200, 250, 300, 350, 400, 450, 500

Practice

1 a 200 **b** 500 **c** 800
  d 100 **e** 400 **f** 700
2 a 800 **b** 250 **c** 1000
  d 450 **e** 200 **f** 100
3 to **8** Answers will vary

Week 7, Lesson 3 – Page 33

Refresher

1 a 7+3+5=**15** **b** 9+3+7=**19**
  c 5+4+6=**15** **d** 2+8+7=**17**
  e 6+6+5=**17** **f** 10+11+5=**26**
2 a 7+**8**+4=19 **b** 5+8+**7**=20
  c 9+6+**6**=21

Practice

a Total = 15

4	9	2
3	5	7
8	1	6

b Total = 21

6	5	10
11	7	3
4	9	8

c Total = 24

5	10	9
12	8	4
7	6	11

d Total = 36

13	14	9
8	12	16
15	10	11

e Total = 42

15	16	11
10	14	18
17	12	13

f Total = 117

38	43	36
37	39	41
42	35	40

Week 7, Lesson 4 – Page 34

Refresher

Answers will vary

Practice

Answers will vary

Week 7, Lesson 5 – Page 35

Refresher

1 a 10 **b** 12 **c** 16
  d 16 **e** 13 **f** 19
  g 13
2 a 6+2+1 = 9 **b** 4+3+2 = 9
  c 6+3+1 = 10 **d** 4+5+1 = 10
  e 6+4+1 = 11

Practice

Answers will vary

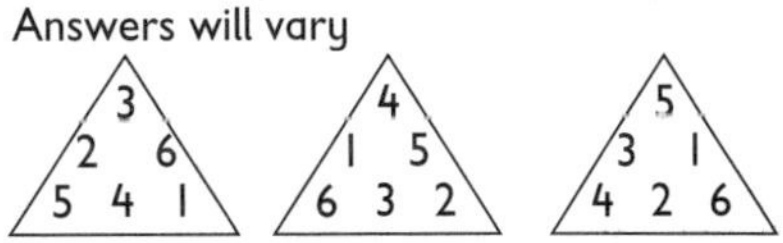

Week 8, Lesson 1 – Page 36

Refresher

1 3 are left

2a 10 **b** 30 **c** 14 **d** 9 **e** 27
f 10 **g** 6 **h** 5 **i** 5 **j** 3

Practice

1

	40, 10	12, 32
10, 35	20, 20	8, 4
25, 15	60, 30	20, 16
30, 25	40, 90	40, 20
40, 35	50, 80	36, 40

2

16 ÷ 5 = 3 (r1)	12 ÷ 5 = 2 (r2)
27 ÷ 5 = 5 (r2)	33 ÷ 5 = 6 (r3)
41 ÷ 5 = 8 (r1)	52 ÷ 5 = 10 (r2)
36 ÷ 5 = 7 (r1)	19 ÷ 5 = 3 (r4)
29 ÷ 5 = 5 (r4)	37 ÷ 5 = 7 (r2)
43 ÷ 10 = 4 (r3)	27 ÷ 10 = 2 (r7)
62 ÷ 10 = 6 (r2)	45 ÷ 10 = 4 (r5)
51 ÷ 10 = 5 (r1)	16 ÷ 10 = 1 (r6)
24 ÷ 10 = 2 (r4)	35 ÷ 10 = 3 (r5)
96 ÷ 10 = 9 (r6)	82 ÷ 10 = 8 (r2)
13 ÷ 4 = 3 (r1)	9 ÷ 4 = 2 (r1)
23 ÷ 4 = 5 (r3)	42 ÷ 4 = 10 (r2)
37 ÷ 4 = 9 (r1)	34 ÷ 4 = 8 (r2)
6 ÷ 4 = 1 (r2)	17 ÷ 4 = 4 (r1)
21 ÷ 4 = 5 (r1)	43 ÷ 4 = 10 (r3)

Week 8, Lesson 2 – Page 37

Refresher

a 25 ÷ 5 = 5 **b** 11 ÷ 2 = 5 (r1)
c 30 ÷ 5 = 6 **d** 30 ÷ 10 = 3
e 22 ÷ 5 = 4 (r2) **f** 22 ÷ 3 = 7 (r1)
g 16 ÷ 4 = 4 **h** 43 ÷ 10 = 4 (r3)
i 76 ÷ 10 = 7 (r6) **j** 12 ÷ 3 = 4
k 16 ÷ 5 = 3 (r1) **l** 43 ÷ 4 = 10 (r3)
m 20 ÷ 2 = 10 **n** 10 ÷ 3 = 3 (r1)
o 17 ÷ 2 = 8 (r1)

Practice

a 16 ÷ 5 = 3 (r1)
You need 4 cars

b 46 ÷ 5 = 9 (r1)
I can buy 9 tickets

c 38 ÷ 5 = 7 (r3)
I need 8 boxes

d 27 ÷ 4 = 6 (r3)
7 tables are needed

e 16 ÷ 3 = 5 (r1)
I can buy 5 packets of balloons

f 46 ÷ 4 = 11 (r2)
11 sweets each ($11\frac{1}{2}$ sweets is acceptable)

Week 8 , Lesson 3 – Page 38

Refresher

1 a 80 ÷ 10 = 8p
b 30 ÷ 3 = 10p 10p × 2 = 20p
c 40 ÷ 5 = 8p **d** 12 ÷ 2 = 6p
e 25 ÷ 5 = 5p 2 × 5p = 10p

Practice

a 45 ÷ 5 = 9 nine days
b 80 ÷ 10 = 8 eight days
c 35 ÷ 5 = 7 7 oranges taken per day
d 50 ÷ 5 = 10 10 × 10 = 100
10 strawberries = £1
8 × 10 = 80
8 strawberries = 80p

e 40 ÷ 8 = 5 2 × 5 = 10
2 tomatoes = 10p
6 × 5 = 30
6 tomatoes = 30p

f 35 ÷ 5 = 7 3 × 7 = 21
3 bananas = 21p
10 × 7 = 70
10 bananas = 70p

Week 8, Lesson 4 – Page 39

Refresher

1 a 1, 7, 6, 5, 4, 8, 3, 2, 9
b 30, 20, 50, 80, 40, 90, 60, 20, 10
c 400, 900, 800, 300, 600, 200, 500, 700, 100

Practice

1a 400 **b** 50 **c** 7
d 300 **e** 40 **f** 500

2a 10 × 9p = 90p
b 10 × 6p = 60p
c 100 × 8p = 800p or £8
d 100 × 7p = 700p or £7
e 100 × 8p = 800p or £8
f 100 × £4 = £400

g 1×6p=6p
h 1×7p=7p
i 10×£4=£40

Week 8, Lesson 5 – Page 40

Refresher

70×10=700 20×10=200 80×10=800
700÷10=70 200÷10=20 800÷10=80
90×10=900 6×100=600 3×100=300
900÷10=90 600÷100=6 300÷100=3
5×100=500 500÷100=5

Practice

£800÷10=£80 £900÷10=£90
£300÷10=£30 £400÷10=£40
£600÷10=£60 £500÷10=£50
£200÷10=£20

2 a 3 **b** 40 **c** 7 **d** 9 **e** 50
f 8 **g** 4 **h** 20 **i** 6

Week 9, Lesson 1 – Page 41

Refresher

1 2×2=4 1×2=2 11×2=22
9×2=18 8×2=16 7×2=14
6×2=12 14×2=28 12×2=24
4×2=8 13×2=26 5×2=10
3×2=6 15×2=30 16×2=32
10×2=20 2÷2=1 16÷2=8
24÷2=12 12÷2=6 14÷2=7
4÷2=2 22÷2=11 20÷2=10
8÷2=4 10÷2=5 18÷2=9
6÷2=3

Practice

a 80 **b** ×2, 100 **c** 50
d 35, double **e** 20, half **f** 45, ×2
g 15, ×2 **h** ÷2, 30, ×2
i double, 70, half
(Note: Some of these answers will vary)

Week 9, Lesson 2 – Page 42

Refresher

3×3=9 5×3=15 4×3=12
3×2=6 4×5=20 3×4=12
5×5=25 1×3=3

Practice

1 a 20 60 80
100 120
b 150 200 50
250 100
c 150 30 120
90 60
d 160 120 40
80 200
e 100 400 200
500 300
f 10 20 30
40 50

Week 9, Lesson 3 – Page 43

Refresher

1 a 2×20p=40p **b** 2×3p=6p
c 2×40p=80p **d** 2×30p=60p
e 2×4p=8p
2 a 3×3p=9p **b** 3×20p=60p
c 3×30p=90p **d** 3×2p=6p
e 3×10p=30p

Practice

1 a 2×23p=46p 2×20=40
2×3=6 40+6=46
b 3×23p=69p 3×20=60
3×3=9 60+9=69
2 a 3×12p=36p 3×10=30
3×2=6 30+6=36
b 4×12p=48p 4×10=40
4×2=8 40+8=48
3 a 3×32p=96p 3×30=90
3×2=6 90+6=96
b 4×32p=128p 4×30=120
4×2=8 120+8=128
4 a 3×33p=99p 3×30=90
3×3=9 90+9=99
b 2×33p=66p 2×30=60
2×3=6 60+6=66

Week 9, Lesson 4 – Page 44

Refresher

a 12 **b** 90 **c** 45
d 12 **e** 160 **f** 35

g 36 h 100 i 20
j 35 k 30 l 80
m 100 n 96 o 6
p 200 q 84 r 90

Practice

1 a $23 \times 3 = 69$ 69 cakes altogether
b $24 \div 2 = 12$ 12 children
c $30 \div 3 = 10$ 10 rocks in each box
d $240 \div 2 = 120$ 120 balls are not flat
e $50 \div 2 = 25$ They jogged for 25 km
f $100 \times 6 = 600$ They spend £600
g $800 \div 10 = 80$ 80 crayons per box
h $45 \times 2 = 90$ The journey is 90 miles

Week 9, Lesson 5 – Page 45

Refresher

1 a 9×3 b $10 \div 5$ c 9×3
d 10×5 e 50×10 f 24×2

Practice

1 27, 2, 27, 50, 500, 48

2 a $90 \div 2 = 45$ We got 45p each
b $46 \div 5 = 9$ (r1) I can buy 9 tickets
c $50 \times 5 = 250$ I bought 250 balloons altogether
d $450 \times 2 = 900$ No
e $3 \times 33 = 99$ £1 – 99p = 1p Jim gets 1p change
f $28 \div 5 = 5$ (r3) They need 2 more children

Week 10, Lesson 1 – Page 46

Refresher

a $\frac{1}{2}$ b $\frac{1}{4}$ c $\frac{3}{4}$
d 1 e $1\frac{1}{2}$ f $2\frac{1}{4}$

Practice

1 Missing fractions – $\frac{1}{2}$, $\frac{3}{4}$, $1\frac{1}{2}$, $1\frac{3}{4}$, $2\frac{1}{4}$, $2\frac{1}{2}$, $3\frac{1}{4}$, $3\frac{1}{2}$, $3\frac{3}{4}$, $4\frac{1}{4}$, $4\frac{1}{2}$, $4\frac{3}{4}$

2 a $\frac{3}{4}$ b $1\frac{1}{4}$ c $1\frac{3}{4}$
d 3 e $4\frac{3}{4}$ f 4

3 a $\frac{1}{2}$ b $1\frac{1}{2}$ c $\frac{3}{4}$
d $\frac{1}{4}$ e $2\frac{3}{4}$ f $4\frac{1}{2}$

4 Answers will vary

Week 10, Lesson 2 – Page 47

Refresher

a $\frac{2}{5}$ b $\frac{3}{5}$ c $\frac{1}{5}$ d $\frac{4}{5}$ e $1\frac{1}{5}$ f $1\frac{2}{5}$

Practice

1 missing numbers – $\frac{1}{5}$, $\frac{3}{5}$, $1\frac{2}{5}$, $1\frac{4}{5}$, $2\frac{1}{5}$, $2\frac{3}{5}$, $2\frac{4}{5}$, $3\frac{1}{5}$, $3\frac{2}{5}$, $3\frac{3}{5}$, $3\frac{4}{5}$, $4\frac{1}{5}$, $4\frac{2}{5}$, $4\frac{3}{5}$, $4\frac{4}{5}$

2 a $\frac{2}{5}$ b $\frac{3}{5}$ c $1\frac{2}{5}$ d $2\frac{4}{5}$

3 a $\frac{2}{5}$ b $\frac{1}{5}$ c $\frac{3}{5}$ d $\frac{4}{5}$

4 Answers will vary

Week 10, Lesson 3 – Page 48

Refresher

a $\frac{1}{2}$ b $\frac{3}{4}$ c $\frac{1}{4}$ d $\frac{1}{4}$

Practice

1 a $\frac{1}{4}$ b $\frac{1}{2}$ c $\frac{2}{3}$
d $\frac{3}{4}$ e $\frac{1}{4}$ f $\frac{1}{2}$

2 a 7:35 b 2:10 c 12:00 d 9:50

Week 10, Lesson 4 – Page 49

Refresher

1 a 40 b 20 c 50 d 25

2 a 20 b 40 c 16 d 24

Practice

Open

Week 10, Lesson 5 – Page 50

Refresher

1 a 18 b 31 c 47 d 27

2 a 26 b 54 c 82 d 64

Practice

1 a 54 cm b 158 cm
c 72 cm d 252 cm

2 a 23 cm b 48.5 cm
c 109 cm d 226.5 cm

3 a 21 cm b 13 cm (approx.)
c 37 cm d 90 cm (approx.)

Week 11, Lesson 1 – Page 51

Refresher

Open

Practice

Open

Week 11, Lesson 2 – Page 52

Refresher

a 22	**b** 23	**c** 24	**d** 24
e 32	**f** 33	**g** 28	**h** 19
I 37	**j** 48	**k** 48	**l** 29
m 14	**n** 26	**o** 9	

Practice

a 46	**b** 38	**c** 36	**d** 122
e 118	**f** 129	**g** 142	**h** 136
i 82	**j** 92	**k** 92	**l** 78
m 58	**n** 77	**o** 87	

Week 11, Lesson 3 – Page 53

Refresher

a 19	**b** 28	**c** 28
d 27	**e** 24	**f** 44
g 58	**h** 48	**i** 46

Practice

a 148	**b** 128	**c** 155	**d** 146
e 159	**f** 83	**g** 91	**h** 71
i 74	**j** 87		

Week 11, Lesson 4 – Page 54

Refresher

Answers will vary

Practice

1 a Wednesday
b Tuesday
c Thursday

2 a 03.08.01 **b** 28.08.01
c 16.08.01 **d** 12.08.01

3 a Tuesday **b** 01.09.01

4 a 4 times **b** Answers will vary

Week 11, Lesson 5 – Page 55

Refresher

Minutes	Time
0	2:15pm
15	2:30pm
5	**2:35pm**
25	**3:00pm**
10	3:10pm
15	**3:25pm**
35	**4:00pm**
10	**4:10pm**
5	4:15pm

Practice

1

	Gatwick South	Gatwick North	Heathrow Terminal 4	Heathrow Central
Service A	9:00	9: 05	9: 55	10: 10
Service B	9:10	9:15	10: 05	10:20
Service C	9: 20	9: 25	10:15	10: 30

2 a 5 minutes
b 1 hour 5 minutes
c 55 minutes

3 They will arrive at Heathrow Central at 12.00pm

Week 12, Lesson 1 – Pages 56 & 57

Refresher

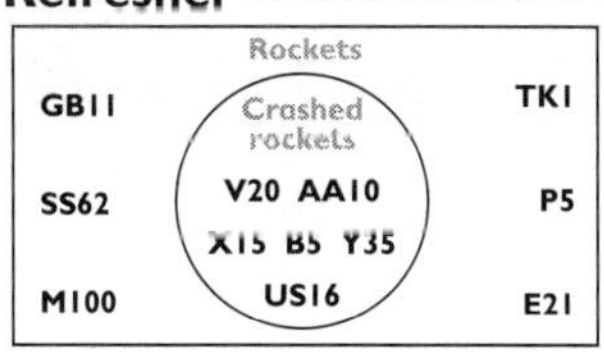

3 6 rockets have crashed

Practice

1 SS62, M100, V20, AA10, US16

2

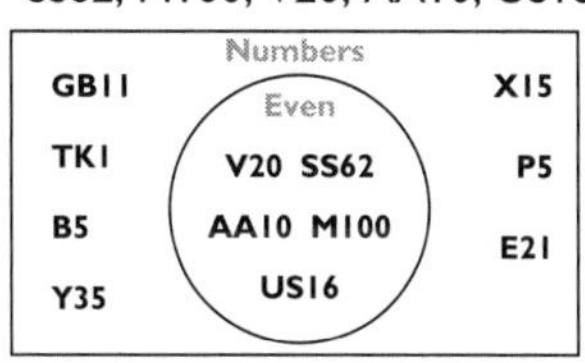

3 7 rockets do not have even numbers

Week 12, Lesson 2– Pages 58 & 59

Refresher

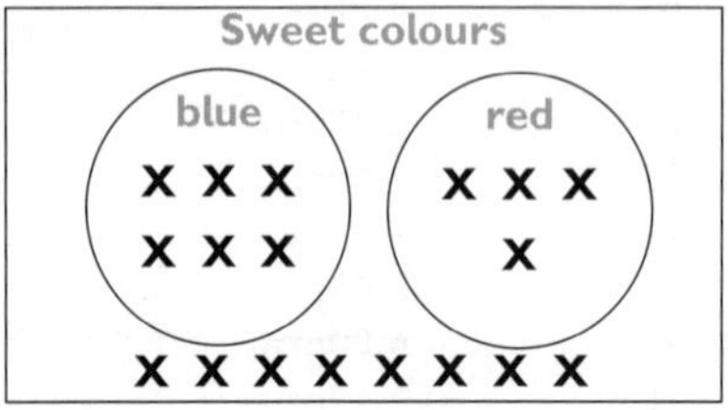

3 4 sweets are red

4 10 sweets are red or blue

Practice

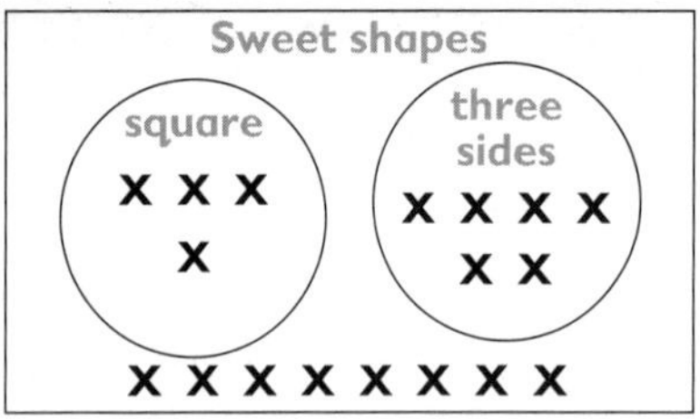

3 6 sweets have three sides

4 14 sweets are not squares

5 Sweets that are not square or triangular

Week 12, Lesson 3 – Page 60 & 61

Refresher

Parachute numbers	
Even	**Not even**
40 34 6	59 305
18 72	37 63 83
124 500	21 17

3 7 numbers are even

4 7 numbers are not even

Practice

Odd numbers up to 20	
One digit	**More than one digit**
1	11 13
3 7	15 17
5	19
9	

Multiples of 5 up to 100			
Odd		**Not odd**	
5	15	10	20
25	35	30	40
45	55	50	60
65	75	70	80
85	95	90	100

5 10 multiples of 5 are odd

6 10 multiples of 5 are not odd

Week 12, Lesson 4 –Pages 62 & 63

Refresher

Open

Practice

Open

Week 12, Lesson 5 – Page 64

Refresher

3 Red seashells–7
Blue seashells–4
Red and blue seashells–5

4 7 seashells are only red.

5 5 seashells are red and blue.

Practice

2 & 3 8 striped fish, 9 dotted fish, 10 striped / dotted fish

4 8 fish are striped

5 10 fish are striped and dotted

6 8 fish are not dotted

Answers

Support Copymasters

Autumn

SCM 1

1 a one b two c three
d 4 e five f 6
g seven h 8 i nine
j 10 k eleven l 12
m thirteen n 14 o fifteen
p 16 q seventeen r 18
s nineteen t 20

2 a thirty b 40 c fifty
d 60 e seventy f 80
g ninety h hundred

3 a 200 b three hundred
c 400 d five hundred
e 600 f seven hundred
g 800 h nine hundred
i thousand

SCM 2

SCM 3

12+6=**18** 25+4=**29** 32+7=**39**
23+5=**28** 44+6=**50** 51+3=**54**
64+4=**68** 42+8=**50** 31+9=**40**
40+7=**47**

SCM 4

a 33 b 24 c 28
d 55 e 83 f 43
g 93 h 59 i 76
j 61

SCM 5

a 38−13=**25** b 46+12=**58**
c 56+14=**70** d 43−11=**32**
e 67+15=**82** f 55−14=**41**
g 85+16=**101** h 78−15=**63**
i 92+11=**103** j 65−17=**48**

SCM 6

1 30p+**30p**=**60p**
2 20p+50p=**70p**
3 20p
4 4 weeks
5 **70p**+**50p**+**30p**=**£1.50**

SCM 7

1 3m 50 cm
$7\frac{1}{2}$m
11m 50 cm
$2\frac{1}{2}$m

2 4m 50 cm
6.5 m
10 m 50 cm
9.5 m

3 $5\frac{1}{2}$ m
$3\frac{1}{2}$ m
$8\frac{1}{2}$ m
$12\frac{1}{2}$ m

SCM 8

1 Open

2 a The **orange** shapes are rectangular prisms.
b The **green** shapes are square prisms.
c The **yellow** shapes are hexagonal prisms.
d The **blue** shapes are triangular prisms.

SCM 9

Prism Packers – a, b, c, g, h
Five Faces – c
Right-angled Roadsters – a, b, g
Curved Carriers – d, e, f, i

SCM 10

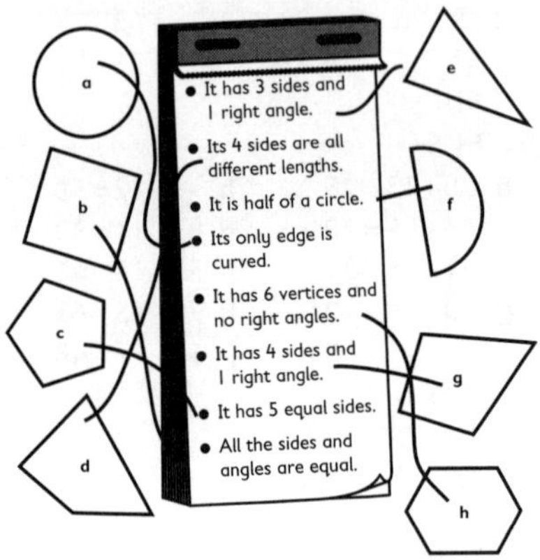

all right angles	some right angles	no right angles
b	e, g	a, c, d, f, h

SCM 11

Open

SCM 12

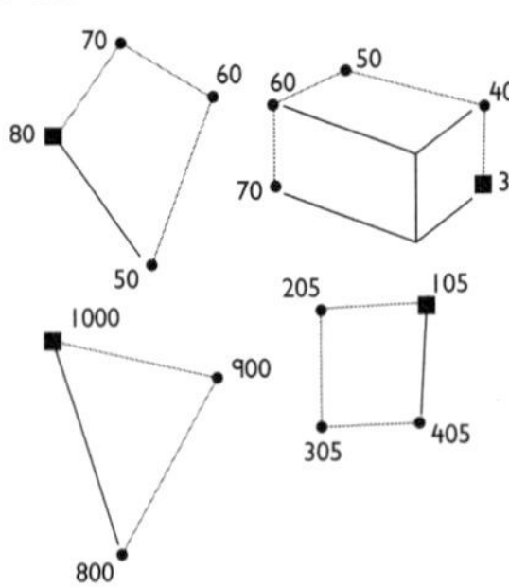

SCM 13

Open

SCM 14

1

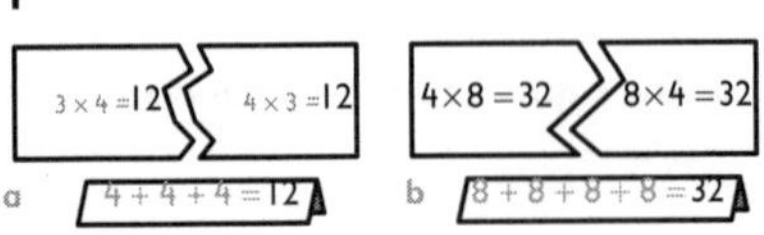

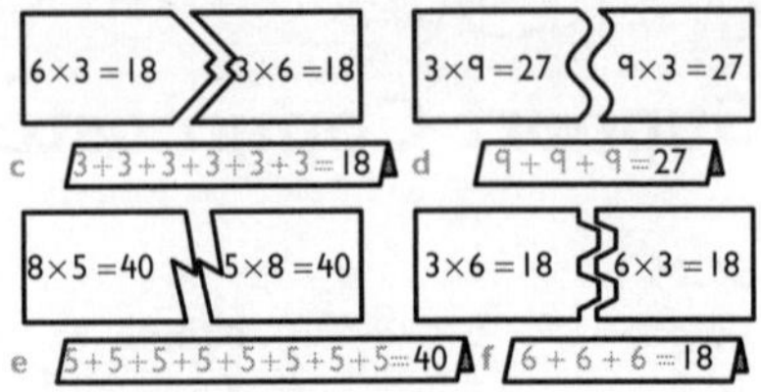

2 Answers will vary

SCM 15

Open

SCM 16

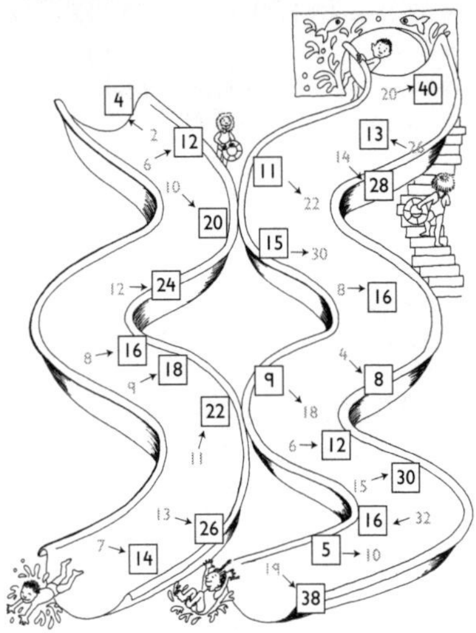

SCM 17

1

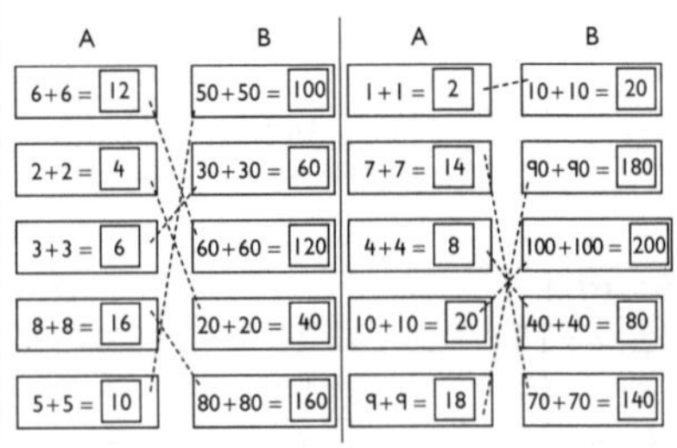

2 a 20, 25, 30, 35, **40**, **45**, **50**, **55**, **60**

b 50, 100, 150, 200, **250**, **300**, **350**, **400**, **450**

c 100, 95, **90**, **85**, 80, **75**, **70**, **65**, 60

d 50, **100**, **150**, 200, 250, 300, **350**, **400**, **450**

e 400, 350, 300, 250, **200**, **150**, **100**, **50**, **0**

SCM 18

Answers will vary

SCM 19

Answers will vary

SCM 20

1 b **5**+**3**=8
8−**3**=**5**
or 8 − 5 = 3

c 7+4=11
11−4=7
or 11 − 7 = 4

d 10+6=16
16−6=10
or 16 − 10 = 6

e 8+5=13
13−5=8
or 13 − 8 = 5

f 4+12=16
16−4=12
or 16 − 12 = 4

g 11+6=17
17−6=11
or 17 − 11 = 6

h 9+10=19
19−9=10
or 19 − 10 = 9

SCM 21

a 23 − 18 = **5**				
b 32 − 27 = **5**	**33**	32	**31**	30
	29	28	**27**	26
c 35 − 29 = **6**	**35**	**34**	**33**	32
	31	**30**	29	
d 41 − 36 − 5	**42**	41	**40**	**39**
	38	37	**36**	
e 43 − 39 = **4**	**43**	**42**	**41**	40
	39	38	**37**	
f 54 − 48 = **6**	**54**	**53**	**52**	**51**
	50	49	**48**	**47**

SCM 22

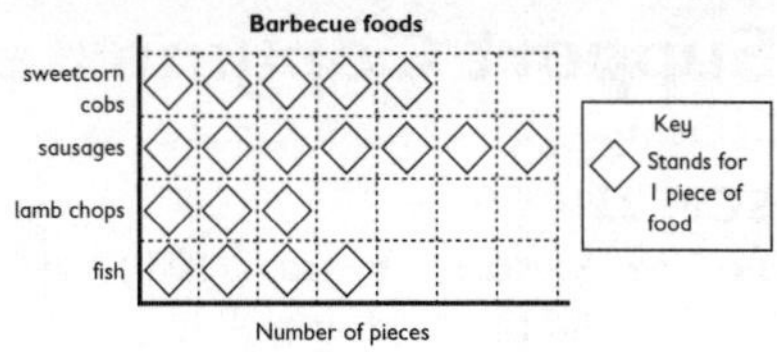

3 a 5 b 3 c 4

d Sausages e 19 f 3

Answers

Support Copymasters

Spring

SCM 23

1 a Joe (second) b Liam (10th)
c Paul (fifth) d Mei (8th)
e Ann (eleventh) f Dem (3rd)
g Hannah (12th) h Deb (sixth)
i Sam (4th)

2 Sam 4th, Deb 6th, Mei 8th, Pip 9th, Ann 11th, Hannah 12th

3 Martin **first**, Joe **second**, Dem **third**, Paul **fifth**, Harry **seventh**, Liam **tenth**

4 first, 1st, second, 2nd, third, 3rd, fourth, 4th, fifth, 5th, sixth, 6th, seventh, 7th, eighth, 8th, ninth, 9th, tenth, 10th, eleventh, 11th, twelfth, 12th, thirteenth, 13th, fourteenth, 14th, fifteenth, 15th, sixteenth, 16th, seventeenth, 17th, eighteenth, 18th, nineteenth, 19th, twentieth, 20th

SCM 24

a 5+0=**5** b 3+**2**=5 c 1+**4**=5
d 5 – **2**=3 e 5 – **4**=1 f 5 – 0=**5**
a 7–3=**4** b 7–**2**=5 c 7–6=**1**
d 7–7=**0** e 2+**5**=7 f 7+**0**=7
g **3**+4=7 h **6**+1=7
a 9+**0**=9 b 9–**4**=5 c 9–**2**=7
d 8+**1**=9 e 4+**5**=9 f **6**+3=9
g 9–3=**6** h 9–1=**8** i 9–**0**=9
j **7**+2=9

SCM 25

a 4+3+1=**8** b 6+3+2=**11**
c 5+1+4=**10** d 6+2+1=**9**
e 7+3+2=**12** f 4+2+4=**10**
g 6+2+4=**12** h 8+5+3=**16**
i 9+1+2=**12** j 7+2+4=**13**

SCM 26

1 100 **200 300 400 500 600 700 800 900** 1000

2 a 700 b 400 c 600 d 200
e 1000 f 100 g 300 h 800

3 a 800 b 1000 c 500 d 300
e 1100 f 700 g 400 h 900

4 a 300, 400, **500**, **600**, 700, 800, 900, **1000**
b 300, **400**, **500**, 600, **700**, **800**, **900**, 1000
c 0, **100**, **200**, 300, **400**, **500**, 600, **700**
d **200**, **300**, 400, **500**, **600**, 700, **800**, 900

SCM 27

1 Mr Pip has 18 apples and oranges to sell.
2 Katie buys 7 pieces of fruit altogether.
3 He will have 5 apples left.
4 He sells 6 pears.
5 He has 5 bananas left.

SCM 28

1 Moonbase 1 has a 1 cube tower and needs 6 cubes altogether.
Moonbase 2 has a 2 cube tower and needs 7 cubes altogether.
Moonbase 3 has a 3 cube tower and needs 8 cubes altogether.

2 (This should have a 4 cube tower and needs 9 cubes altogether)

3 10 cubes

4

cubes for tower	total number of cubes (including moonbase)
1	6
2	7
3	8
4	9
5	10

5 15 cubes altogether

SCM 29

1 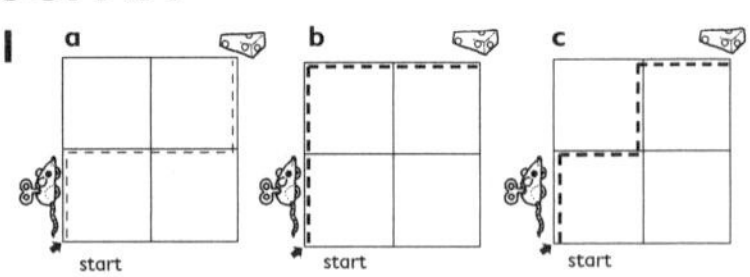

2 Open

SCM 30

1 missing intervals (clockwise) 0, 5, 10, **15**, **20**, **25**, 30, **35**, **40**, **45**, **50**, **55**

2 a Time shown should be 6.40 (am)
b Time shown should be 6.05 (pm)
c Time shown should be 3.55 (pm)
d Time shown should be 9.40 (am)

SCM 31

1 Daisy 5 kg and 500 g or $5\frac{1}{2}$ kg
Dixie 6 kg and 500 g or $6\frac{1}{2}$ kg
Dolly 4 kg and 500 g or $4\frac{1}{2}$ kg

2 Daisy about 12 kg 500 g or about 12.5 kg
Dixie about 13 kg 0 g or about 13 kg
Dolly about 11 kg 500 g or about $11\frac{1}{2}$kg

3

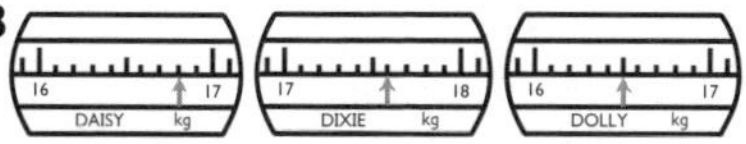

SCM 32

Answers will vary

SCM 33

a 23 26
b 13 17 14 18
c 12 16 13 17
d 23 26 30 27 24
e 9 13 16 12 9
f 30 33 36 40 44 41

SCM 34

1

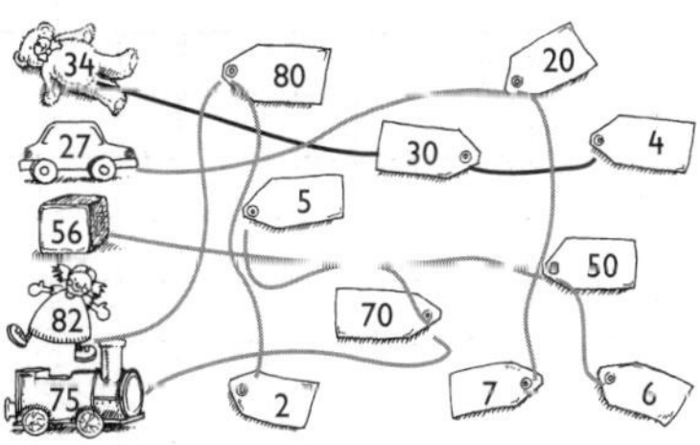

2 a 24=20+4 b 38=**30**+**8**
c 45=**40**+**5** d 62=**60**+**2**
e 71=**70**+**1** f 85=**80**+**5**

3 b 36 b 48 c 57
d 93 e 19 f 86

SCM 35

3 (balls)
How many altogether? 15
How many in each group? 3
How many groups? 5
15÷3=5

(stars)
How many altogether? 16
How many in each group? 4
How many groups? 4
16÷4=4

(shells etc.)
How many altogether? 21
How many in each group? 7
How many groups? 3
21÷7=3

(apples)
How many altogether? 12
How many in each group? 2
How many groups? 6
12÷2=6

(flowers)
How many altogether? 20
How many in each group? 4
How many groups? 5
20÷4=5

(sweets)
How many altogether? 12
How many in each group? 4
How many groups? 5
12÷4=5

SCM 36

1 a 6 in each group b 3 in each group
12÷2=6 15÷5=3
c 2 in each group d 5 in each group
20÷10=2 25÷5=5
e 9 in each group f 4 in each group
18÷2=9 20÷5=4

SCM 37

1 a 5 flowers b 10 crayons c 3 sets
d 5 scoops e 5 cars f 8 fish

SCM 38

1 a fifths $\frac{1}{5}$ b quarters $\frac{1}{4}$ c thirds $\frac{1}{3}$
d fifths $\frac{1}{5}$ e halves $\frac{1}{2}$ f tenths $\frac{1}{10}$

2 Answers will vary

SCM 39

Answers will vary

SCM 40

1 Brontosaurus–4, Tyrannosaurus–3
Pterodactyl–6, Stegosaurus–7

2 4 3 Pterodactyl
4 Stegosaurus 5 3

Answers

Support Copymasters

SCM 41

1 a 91 b 520
c 462 d 330

2 a 605 b 391
c 750 d 521

3 153, 154, 155, **156**, **157**, 158, **159**, **160**, 161, **162**, **163**

4 a 123
b 347, 395, 493, 582
c 275, 347, 395, 493

5 117, 293, 327, 458, 484, 535, 619

SCM 42

1 a 15 b 45 c 40
d 17 e 52 f 63
g 26 h 38 i 78
j 33 k 75 l 84

2 a 4 b 24 c 42
d 9 e 42 f 61
g 16 h 57 i 29
j 11 k 79 l 90

SCM 43

1 a 6 b 9 c 8
16 19 28
d 7 e 8 f 6
17 18 26
g 5 h 9 I 7
15 19 27
j 7 k 9 l 9
17 19 29
m 7 n 5 o 7
17 15 27

SCM 44

1 a 50 b 70
c 100 d 50
e 90 f 80
g 80 h 90

2 a 92 b 73 c 79
d 54 e 94 f 88
g 77 h 86 i 94

3 a 56 b 64 c 78
d 59 e 76 f 78

SCM 45

1 15+9=24p
2 20+9=29p
3 20−15=5p change
4 20+20=40 Oliver needs 40p
5 16−9=7p left

SCM 46

1 Orange 200 ml, Yellow 100 ml, Blue 300 ml, Green 200 ml, Black 400 ml
2 Answers will vary

SCM 47

1

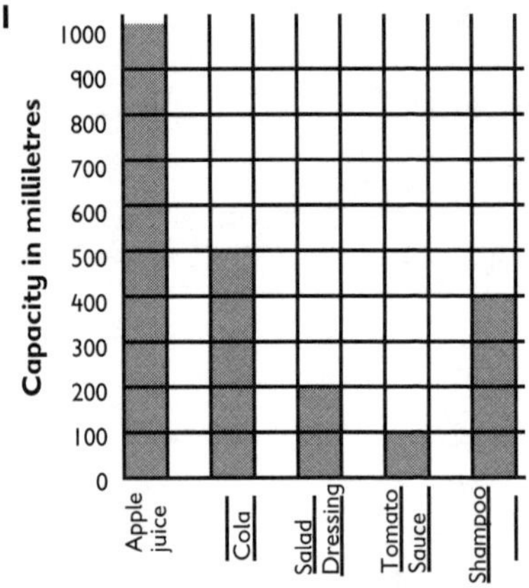

2 a Tomato sauce
b shampoo
c 200ml
d Cola

SCM 48

Open

SCM 49

Open

SCM 50

Less than a right angle – b, c, d

More than a right angle – a, f

SCM 51

Open

SCM 52

Answers will vary

SCM 53

a $16 \div 5 = 3$ (r1) **b** $18 \div 4 = 4$ (r2)
c $23 \div 3 = 7$ (r2) **d** $15 \div 2 = 7$ (r1)
e $24 \div 5 = 4$ (r4) **f** $32 \div 10 = 3$ (r2)
g $26 \div 4 = 6$ (r2) **h** $17 \div 3 = 5$ (r2)

SCM 54

a problem goes with $40 \div 10$
Answer = 4

b problem goes with $18 \div 2$
Answer = 9

c problem goes with $20 \div 5$
Answer = 4

d problem goes with $35 \div 5$
Answer = 7

e problem goes with $12 \div 2$
Answer = 6

SCM 55

1 a $15+15 \rightarrow$ $10+10=20$
$5+5=10$
$20+10=30$
Double $15=30$

b $35+35 \rightarrow$ $30+30=60$
$5+5=10$
$60+10=70$
Double $35=70$

c $40+40 \rightarrow$ $4+4=8$
Double $40=80$

d $20+20 \rightarrow$ $2+2=4$
Double $20=40$

2 a Half of $50 \rightarrow$ $20+20=40$
$5+5=10$
$20+5=25$
Half of $50=25$

b Half of $60 \rightarrow$ $30+30=60$
Half of $60=30$

c Half of $10 \rightarrow$ $5+5=10$
Half of $10=5$

d Half of $20 \rightarrow$ $10+10=20$
Half of $20=10$

SCM 56

(Working round the track clockwise)

$3\times3=9$, $3\times30=90$
$2\times2=4$, $2\times20=40$
$4\times1=4$, $4\times10=40$
$3\times4=12$, $3\times40=120$
$5\times2=10$, $5\times20=100$
$3\times5=15$, $3\times50=150$
$2\times3=6$, $2\times30=60$
$4\times2=8$, $4\times20=80$
$4\times4=16$, $4\times40=160$
$10\times1=10$, $10\times10=100$
$4\times3=12$, $4\times30=120$
$3\times2=6$, $3\times20=60$
$2\times4=8$, $2\times40=80$
$2\times5=10$, $2\times50=100$

SCM 57

1 $\frac{1}{4}, \frac{1}{2}, \frac{3}{4}, 1$

2 $\frac{1}{3}, \frac{2}{3}, 1$

3 $\frac{1}{5}, \frac{2}{5}, \frac{3}{5}, \frac{4}{5}, 1$

SCM 58

1a 10 **b** 8
c 12 **d** 16

2a 8 **b** 20
c 12 **d** 16

3a 50 **b** 30 **c** 40

4a 10 **b** 20 **c** 15

SCM 59

a 17 **b** 22 **c** 22
d 29 **e** 17 **f** 35
g 22 **h** 33 **i** 31

SCM 60

1 fish – 6 bowls

More than 1 fish – 9 bowls

Answers

Extension Copymasters

Autumn

ECM 1

1 a 4 cm **b** 2.4 cm **c** 2 cm
d 3 cm **e** 5 cm **f** 5.5 cm
g 5 cm **h** 4 cm **i** 5 cm
j 4 cm **k** 1.4 cm **l** 3.9 cm

2 Open

ECM 2

1 a

–	9	7	6	8
35	26	28	29	27
53	44	46	47	45
81	72	74	75	73

b

–	5	8	10	7	6	9
92	87	84	82	85	86	83
103	98	95	93	96	97	94
74	69	66	64	67	68	65
82	77	74	72	75	76	73

c

–	9	6	8	5	7	10
51	42	45	43	46	44	41
62	53	56	54	57	55	52
94	85	88	86	89	87	84
86	77	80	78	81	79	76

2 Open

ECM 3

1 a 34+28=**62**
34−28=**6**
b 27+**69**=96
96−**69**=27
c 49+35=**84**
49−35=**14**
d **68**+51=119
119−**68**=51
e 73+**18**=91
91−**18**=73
f 73+89=**162**
89−73=**16**
g 38+49=**87**
49−38=**11**
h 58+**36**=94
94−**36**=58

ECM 4

a £1.72 exchanged for
£1+50p+20p+2p
b £16.72 exchanged for
£10+£5+£1+50p+20p+2p
c £45.50 exchanged for
£20+£20+£5+50p
d £4.63 exchanged for
£2+£2+50p+10p+2p+1p
e £3.95 exchanged for
£2+£1+50p+20p+20p+5p
f £13.78 exchanged for
£10+£2+£1+50p+20p+5p+2p+1p
g £10.04 exchanged for
£10+2p+2p
h £21.46 exchanged for
£20+£1+20p+20p+5p+1p
i £37.08 exchanged for
£20+£10+£5+£2+5p+2p+1p

ECM 5

£12.50 £7.50 Altogether £20.00
£4.30 £20.07 Altogether £24.37
£15.17 £9.60 Altogether £24.77
£12.53 £20.40 Altogether £32.93

ECM 6

a 4p 14p 24p 84p **b** 60p
c Answers will vary e.g.
£3.60 and £3.20 and £2.40 = £9.20
£2.80 and £3.60 and £3.20 = £9.60
£3.20 and £4.40 and £2.40 = £10

ECM 7

1 a f **b** e **c** h **d** d **e** a

2 Ball a 40 cm
Ball b 1 m 80 cm
Ball c 3 m 70 cm

ECM 8

2D shape ➡ / ⬇ prism		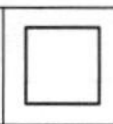	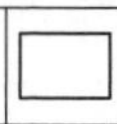	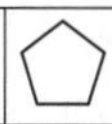	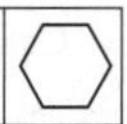
a 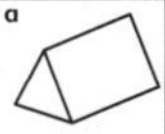	2		3		
b 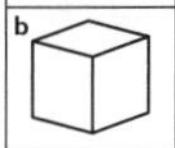		6			
c 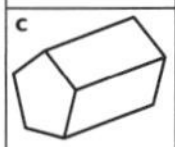			5	2	
d 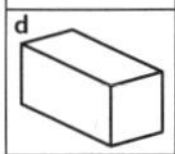		2	4		
e 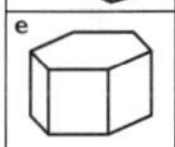			6		2
f 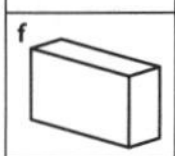			6		

ECM 9

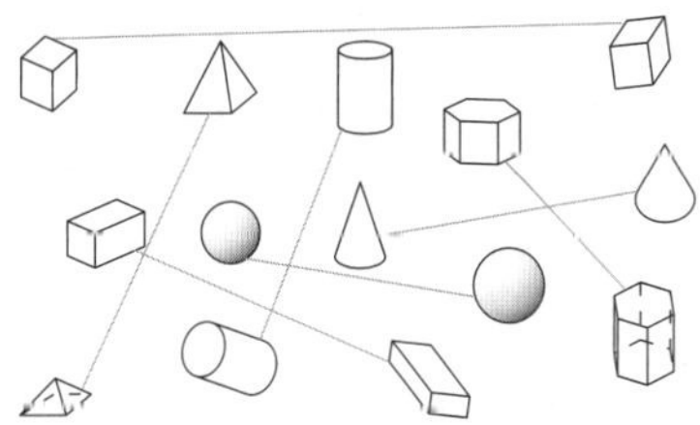

3D shape	At least 5 faces	Identical end faces	Right-angled vertices	Curved face
a cube	yes	yes	yes	no
b cuboid	yes	yes	yes	no
c cone	no	no	no	yes
d cylinder	no	yes	no	yes
e sphere	no	no	no	yes
f hemisphere	no	no	no	yes
g triangular prism	yes	yes	no	no
h hexagonal prism	yes	yes	yes	no
i square base pyramid	yes	no	no	no

ECM 10

a 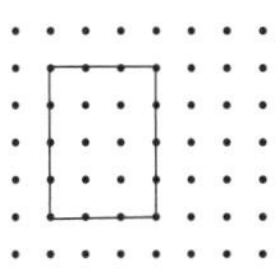

b 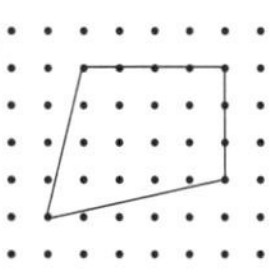

c 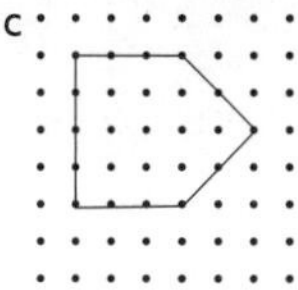

d 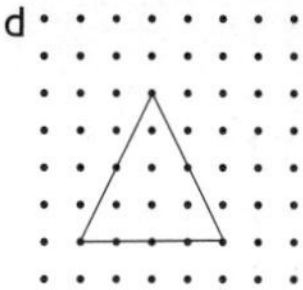

2 a pentagon with 2 right-angled vertices

b 8 vertices, no right angles, 4 pairs of sides of same length

c hexagon with 2 right angled vertices

d right-angled triangle with 2 equal sides

ECM 11

Open

ECM 12

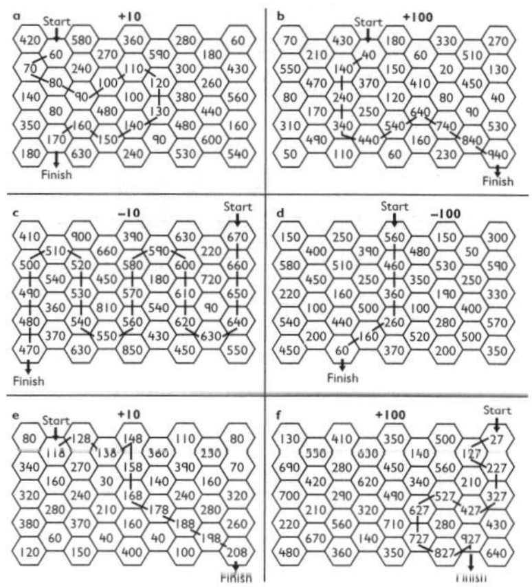

ECM 13

Start	Count → forwards ← backwards	Finish	Odd or Even
75	→ 6	81	Odd
38	← 12	26	Even
26	→ 9	35	Odd
94	→ 8	102	Even
52	← 17	35	Odd
73	← 8	65	Odd
91	→ 9	100	Even
68	→ 16	84	Even
47	← 15	32	Even
212	→ 8	220	Even
177	→ 23	200	Even
129	← 18	111	Odd
364	← 14	350	Even

ECM 14

Open

ECM 15

Verbal answers

ECM 16

a 9×4=36 I bought the board game

b 4×7=28 30−28=2 He has £2 left

c 4×10=40 4×6=24 40−24=16
It costs £16 more to buy the computer games

d 2×9=18 2×4=8 18−8=10
It costs £10 less in the sale

e 4×5=20 7×4=28
Jan spends the most money

f 4×7=28 4×4=16 28−16=12
It cost £12 more / extra

ECM 17

a 8×5=40 8×4=32 40−32=8
It costs £8 more to buy the lemons

b 7×10=70 4×2=8 70−8=62
The difference is £62

c 6×3=18 6×10=60 18+60=78
9×2=18 9×5=45 18+45=63
It costs £15 more to buy the oranges and apples

d 3×3=9 3×10=30 3×4=12
9+30+12=51
5×5=25 5×2=10 25+10=35
Billy spends £16 more

e 8×2=16 It costs £16

f Answers will vary e.g.
5×3=15 5 boxes of oranges
4×10=40 4 boxes of apples
10×4=40 7 boxes of bananas

ECM 18

1a $\frac{4}{5}$ **b** $\frac{2}{4}$ $(\frac{1}{2})$ **c** $\frac{5}{10}$ $(\frac{1}{2})$ **d** $\frac{6}{10}$

2a $\frac{3}{5}$ **b** $\frac{3}{4}$ **c** $\frac{4}{5}$ **d** $\frac{7}{10}$

3a $\frac{2}{10}$ of 30 **6** **b** $\frac{4}{10}$ of 40 **16**

c $\frac{7}{10}$ of 50 **35** **d** $\frac{8}{10}$ of 20 **16**

4 Open

5 Open

ECM 19

1a $\frac{2}{5}$ each **b** $\frac{3}{4}$ each **c** $\frac{2}{4}$ each

2a $1\frac{1}{3}$ **b** $1\frac{1}{4}$

3 Open

ECM 20

a 17−8=**9** 17−**9**=**8**

b 14−9=**5** 14−**5**=**9**

c 19−5=**14** 19−**14**=**5**

d 18−12=**6** 18−**6**=**12**

e 15−13=**2** 15−**2**=**13**

f 16−7=**9** 16−**9**=**7**

g 17−11=**6** 17−**6**=**11**

ECM 21

a 25+37=62 37−25=12
37+25=62 37−12=25

b 59 48+59=107 59−48=11
59+48=107 59−11=48

c 67 67+26=93 67−26=41
26+67=93 67−41=26

d 55 81+55=136 81−55=26
55+81=136 81−26=55

e 150 85+150=235 150−85=65
150+85=235 150−65=85

f 76 76+101=177 101−76=25
101+76=177 101−25=76

g 91 72+91=163 91−72=19
91+72=163 91−19=72

h 83 57+83=140 83−57=26
83+57=140 83−26=57

ECM 22

1

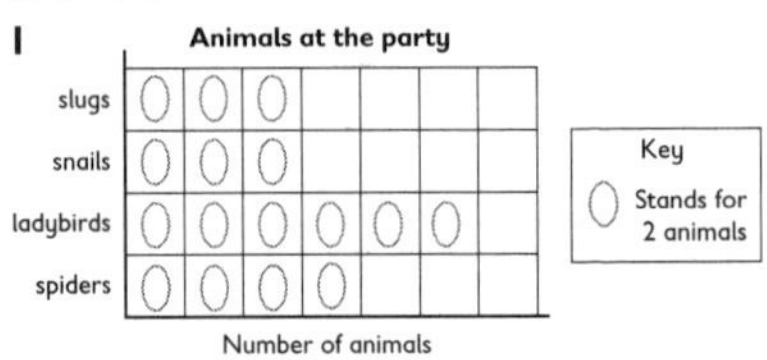

2a 6 **b** 6 **c** 6

d 26 **e** 18

3

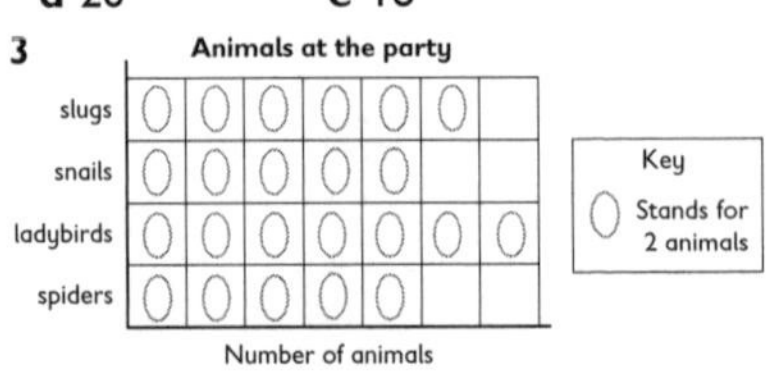

Answers

Extension Copymasters

Spring

ECM 23

1 10 g, 75 g, 700 g, 20 g
25 g, 60 g, 150 g, 1250 g

2

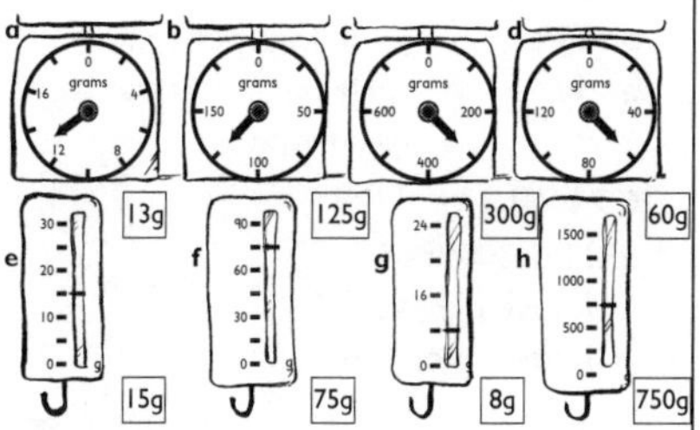

ECM 24

a 13+6+7+4=30 b 6+**23**+5+8=42
c 12+9+**11**+2=34 d 6+**18**+14+5=43
e 23+8+**19**+1=51 f 8+**2**+19+25=54
g 7+4+32+15=**58** h 11+5+**27**+5=48
i **14**+28+6+3=51 j 18+7+3+**36**=64
k 2+23+**23**+9=57 l 16+9+1+**12**=38
m 7+15+2+24=**48** n 3+21+**15**+8=47

ECM 25

a 85+1+5+4=95 86+10−1=95
b 75+3+3+5=86 78+10−2=86
c 65+2+5+9=76 67+10−1=76
d 95+1+5+1=102 96+5+1=102
e 25+3+35+1=64
20+30+8+6=64
f 25+2+25+4=56 27+30−1=56
g 35+3+45+1=84 40+46−2=84
h 25+1+15+3=44 26+20−2=44
i 125+1+25+2=153
126+30−3=153
j 115+3+15+4=137
118+20−1=137

ECM 26

1a 800
300+500=800
600+**200**=800
100+700=800
200+**600**=800
400+400=800

b 500
100+400=500
200+300=500
0+500=500

c 900
0+900=900
100+800=900
200+700=900
300+600=900
400+500=900

d 1300
0+1300=1300
100+1200=1300
200+1100=1300
300+1000=1300
400+900=1300
500+800=1300
600+700=1300

ECM 27

1 £5
2 £7.50
3 £2.44
4 £2, £2, £2, £1, 50p, 5p, 2p

ECM 28

2 Open
3 12 points

ECM 29

1 a A space building of 1 layer needs 8 bricks.
b A space building of 2 layers needs 16 bricks.
c A space building of 3 layers needs 24 bricks.

2 4 layers, 32 bricks
3 40 bricks
4

Number of layers	1	2	3	4	5
Number of bricks	8	16	24	32	40

5 Numbers increase by 8 each time
6 80 bricks

ECM 30

Answers will vary

ECM 31

1 200 g ← 400 g → 800 g
300 g ← 600 g → 1200 g
250 g ← 500 g → 1000 g

2 800 g
700 g 900 g

ECM 32

Open

ECM 33

Open

ECM 34

1 a 17 b 186 c 28 d 40
e 33 f 42 g 9 h 9

ECM 35

1 a 68+76+49+310=503
b 68+76+91+176=411
c 49+310+27+58=444
d 91+27+176+58=352
e 68+310+176+58=612
f 49+91+27+58=225
g 68+49+176+58=351
h 76+310+91+27=504
(Note: these answers may vary as children will choose different combinations)

ECM 36

1 a $10\times2=20$, $9\times5=45$, $3\times10=30$, $4\times5=20$, $8\times2=16$, $10\times9=90$, $5\times8=40$

2a $20\div2=10$, $45\div5=9$, $30\div10=3$, $20\div5=4$, $16\div2=8$, $90\div9=10$, $40\div5=8$

1b $2\times7=14$, $10\times4=40$, $7\times5=35$, $10\times7=70$, $9\times2=18$, $6\times5=30$, $2\times6=12$

2b $14\div2=7$, $40\div4=10$, $35\div5=7$, $70\div7=10$, $18\div2=9$, $30\div5=6$, $12\div6=2$

1c $25\div5=5$, $30\div5=6$, $100\div10=10$, $22\div2=11$, $40\div2=20$, $18\div2=9$, $55\div5=11$

2c $5\times5=25$, $6\times5=30$, $10\times10=100$, $11\times2=22$, $20\times2=40$, $9\times2=18$, $11\times5=55$

ECM 37

1 a $24\div6=4$ She fills 4 boxes
b $16\div4=4$ There are 4 red files
c $30\div6=5$ 5 packs of pencils are needed
d $60\div5=12$ 12 cars are needed
e $36\div4=9$ Each friend gets 9 chocolates
f $35\div5=7$ 7 5p coins
g $24\div4=6$ 6 children per team
h $50\div5=10$ Each piece of string is 10cm long

ECM 38

1 a I have half ✔
I have quarter ✔
I have quarter ✔
b $\frac{1}{4}$ ✗ $\frac{1}{2}$ ✗ $\frac{1}{3}$ ✔
c $\frac{1}{4}$ ✔ $\frac{1}{2}$ ✗
d $\frac{1}{2}$ ✔ $\frac{1}{4}$ ✗
e $\frac{1}{4}$ ✗ $\frac{1}{4}$ ✔ $\frac{1}{2}$ ✔
f half ✔ two quarters ✔

ECM 39

a He has spent $\frac{4}{5}$. Birthday money– $5\times3=$**£15**
b He has spent $\frac{1}{2}$. Birthday money– $2\times2=$**£4**
c He has spent $\frac{2}{3}$. Birthday money– $3\times3=$**£9**
d She has spent $\frac{3}{4}$. Birthday money– $5\times4=$**£20**
e He has spent $\frac{9}{10}$. Birthday money– $3\times10=$**£30**
f He has spent $\frac{4}{5}$. Birthday money– $5\times4=$**£20**
g He has spent $\frac{2}{3}$. Birthday money– $3\times6=$**£18**
h He has spent $\frac{3}{4}$. Birthday money– $4\times6=$**£24**

ECM 40

Open

Answers

Extension Copymasters

Summer

ECM 41

1 **a** 400 ml **b** 800 ml **c** 200 ml
d 900 ml **e** 40 litres **f** 80 litres
g 70 litres **h** 10 litres

2

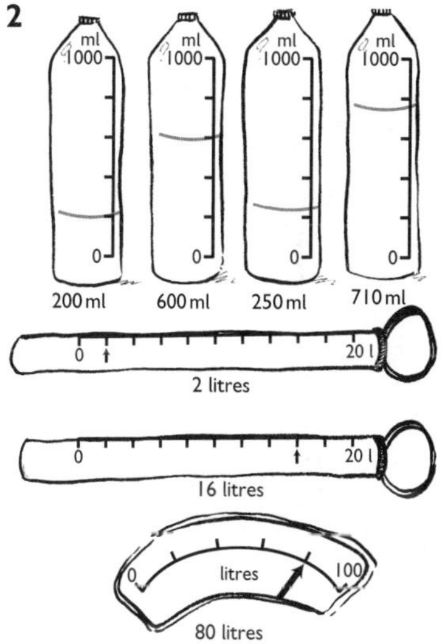

ECM 42

a 17 **b** 75 **c** 59
d 55 **e** 59 **f** 93
g 18 **h** 55 **i** 65
j 21 **k** 63 **l** 31
m 9 **n** 31 **o** 61
p 41 **q** 36 **r** 41
s 19 **t** 51

ECM 43

a 200 **b** 62 **c** 21
d 74 **e** 39 **f** 52
g 900 **h** 71 **I** 52
j 22 **k** 23 **l** 53
m 42 **n** 27 **o** 5
p 41 **q** 32 **r** 31
s 11 **t** 13

ECM 44

Working out will vary

a 269 **b** 359 **c** 597 **d** 495 **e** 695
f 793 **g** 742 **h** 869 **i** 650 **j** 1003

ECM 45

Open

ECM 46

1 Strawberry 250 ml, Lime 150 ml, Lemon 300 ml, Blueberry 700 ml, Orange 450 ml, Raspberry 800 ml

2 Containers should show (left to right): Raspberry 1600 ml, Orange 900 ml, Lemon 600 ml, Blueberry 1400 ml, Strawberry 500 ml, Lime 300 ml

ECM 47

Amount in millilitres	100 ml	200 ml	400 ml	800 ml
100 ml	✔			
200 ml		✔		
300 ml	✔	✔		
400 ml			✔	
500 ml	✔		✔	
600 ml		✔	✔	
700 ml	✔	✔	✔	
800 ml				✔
900 ml	✔			✔
1000 ml		✔		✔
1100 ml	✔	✔		✔
1200 ml			✔	✔
1300 ml	✔		✔	✔
1400 ml		✔	✔	✔
1500 ml	✔	✔	✔	✔

ECM 48

Open

ECM 49

Open

ECM 50

Open

(3c It is a right angle)

ECM 51

1 a 271 should be 270
b 305 should be 310
c 402 should be 405
d 740 should be 732

2 a Multiples of 2 – 370, 426, 494, 338
Multiples of 5 – 370, 465, 335
b Multiples of 5 – 600, 215, 650, 430, 910, 365
Multiples of 10 – 600, 430, 910, 650
c Multiples of 2 – 372, 460, 364, 540, 298, 892
Multiples of 10 – 460, 540
d Multiples of 2 – 312, 316, 314, 310, 306, 308
Multiples of 5 – 315, 310, 305

ECM 52

1

2	7	9	
0	5	1	6
	3	8	4

2

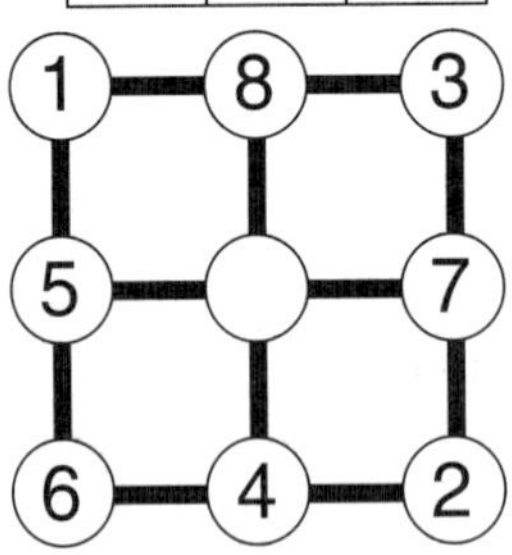

ECM 53

1 a 37÷5=7 (r2)　46÷4=11 (r2)
32÷4=8　53÷5=10 (r3)
27÷3=9　33÷10=3 (r3)
b 17÷4=4 (r1)　27÷2=13 (r1)
35÷3=11 (r2)　28÷4=7
49÷5=9 (r4)　53÷10=5 (r3)
c 89÷10=8 (r9)　46÷2=23
39÷3=13　26÷5=5 (r1)
73÷10=7 (r3)　62÷2=31

2 a 15÷2=7 (r1) 8 cars are needed
b 7÷2=3 (r1) He can buy 3 bags
c 16÷3=5 (r1) She can go on the roller coaster 5 times
d 49÷5=9 (r4) 10 bags are needed
e 29÷4=7 (r1) 8 cars are needed
f 25÷3=8 (r1) He can go on 8 rides

ECM 54

Open

ECM 55

a

Buy	×13
2	**26**
3	**39**
1	**13**

b

Buy	×32
2	**64**
3	**96**
1	**32**

c

Buy	×23
2	**46**
3	**69**
1	**23**

d

Buy	×33
2	**66**
3	**99**
1	**33**

e

Buy	×12
2	**24**
3	**36**
1	**12**

f

Buy	×11
2	**22**
3	**33**
1	**11**

ECM 56

a ×
4×22=88
He spent 88p

b ×
35×10=350
He spent £350

c ÷
90÷2=45
She can buy 45 envelopes

d ×
450×2=900
The box is worth £9

e ÷
450÷10=45
He can buy 45 phonecards

f ×
7×5=35
35 phonecards are sold

g ×
4×12=48
She bought 48 stamps

h × +
3×13=39
3×2=6
3×22=66
39+6=45
45+66=111
She spent £1.11

ECM 57

1 a $\frac{8}{10}$ **b** $\frac{2}{10}$ **c** $\frac{1}{2}$ (or $\frac{5}{10}$)
d $1\frac{3}{10}$ **e** $1\frac{7}{10}$ **f** $2\frac{1}{10}$

2 Missing numbers from numberline:
$\frac{1}{10}$, $\frac{2}{10}$, $\frac{4}{10}$, $\frac{5}{10}$, $\frac{7}{10}$, $\frac{8}{10}$, $\frac{9}{10}$, $1\frac{1}{10}$, $1\frac{3}{10}$, $1\frac{4}{10}$, $1\frac{5}{10}$

3 a $\frac{7}{10}$ **b** $\frac{9}{10}$ **c** 1
d $1\frac{3}{10}$ **e** $2\frac{6}{10}$ **f** $2\frac{1}{10}$

4 Answers will vary

5 a $\frac{4}{10}$ **b** $\frac{7}{10}$
c $1\frac{1}{2}$ **d** $\frac{9}{10}$

ECM 58

1 a $\frac{1}{3}$ **b** $\frac{1}{3}$ **c** $\frac{2}{3}$

2 a $\frac{4}{5}$ **b** $\frac{3}{5}$ **c** $\frac{1}{5}$
d $\frac{2}{5}$ **e** $\frac{3}{5}$ **f** $\frac{2}{5}$

3 Answers will vary

ECM 59

1 a 121 **b** 221
c 258 **d** 405
e 379 **f** 379
g 277 **h** 279
i 486 **j** 92

ECM 60

Answers

Homework Copymasters

Autumn

HCM 1

Refresher

17

Practice

Open

HCM 2

Refresher

6+32=38 43+5=48
4+55=59 23+7=30

Practice

45+10=55 4+58=62 74+20=94
25+40=65 9+45=54 37+50=87

HCM 3

Refresher

a 5+5=10 6+5=**11** 5+4=**9**
b 10+10=20 11+10=**21** 9+10=**19**
c 6+6=12 7+6=**13** 8+6=**14**
d 50+50=100 51+50=**101** 49+50=**99**
e 20+20=40 19+20=**39** 21+20=**41**
f 7+7=14 7+5=**12** 7+8=**15**

Practice

a 30+30=60 29+30=**59** 31+32=**63**
b 25+25=50 23+24=**47** 26+27=**53**
c 12+12=24 13+11=**24** 14+13=**27**
d 35+35=70 34+36=**70** 35+37=**72**
e 45+45=90 43+46=**89** 44+47=**91**
f 100+100=200 98+101=**199** 103+102=**205**

HCM 4

Refresher

£2.20 or 220p £5.50 or 550p
£1.05 or 105p £1.12 or 112p
£2.30 or 230p

Practice

£6.10 or 610p £7.25 or 725p
£10.30 or 1030p £8.55 or 855p
£15.54 or 1554p

HCM 5

Refresher

a 12 tins **b** 36 cards **c** 21 petals

Practice

a 9 cakes **b** 32 sandwiches
c 5 people

HCM 6

Refresher

A is about 3 cm long
B is about 7 cm long
C is about 9 cm long
D is about 14 cm long
E is about 17 cm long
F is about 19 cm long

Practice

a Candle F is about **16 cm** longer than candle A
b Candle E is about **8 cm** longer than candle C
c Candle B is about **7 cm** shorter than candle D
d Candle A is about **14 cm** shorter than candle E

HCM 7

Refresher

a m **b** m **c** cm
d cm **e** cm

Practice

Open

HCM 8

Open – answers will vary according to cartons chosen by the children

HCM 9

Refresher

Open

Practice

HCM 10

Open

HCM 11

Refresher

- **a** 127 – 100 = **27**
- **b** 371 – 100 = **271**
- **c** 371 – 10 = **361**
- **d** 235 + 100 = **335**
- **e** 12 + 10 = **22**
- **f** 455 – 10 = **445**
- **g** 360 – 100 = **260**
- **h** 45 + 10 = **55**
- **i** 67 – 10 = **57**
- **j** 452 + 100 = **552**
- **k** 260 – 10 = **250**
- **l** 670 – 100 = **570**

Practice

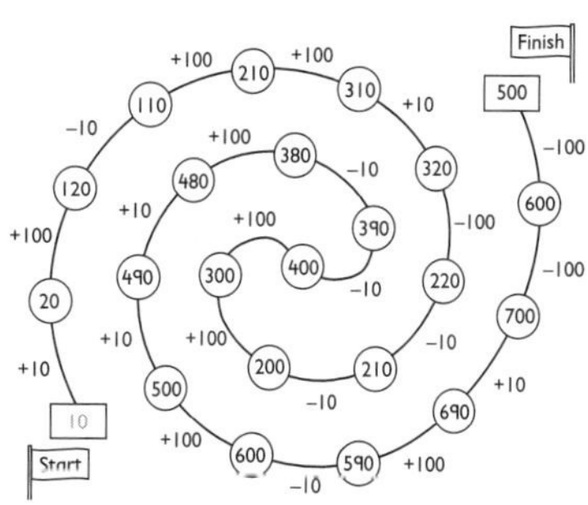

HCM 12

Refresher

Open

Practice

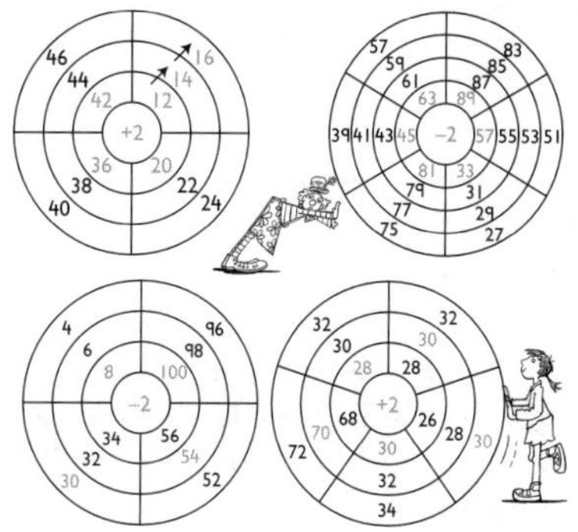

HCM 13

Refresher

a

35	15	10	40	5
30	25	45	20	50

b

8	2	14	10	18
20	4	12	16	6

c

60	20	30	70	100
80	50	10	90	40

Practice

a

×	2	5	10
3	6	15	30
4	8	20	40
6	12	30	60
7	14	35	70
8	16	40	80
9	18	45	90

b

×	2	5	3	6	10	0
2	4	10	6	12	20	16
5	10	25	15	30	50	40
10	20	50	30	60	100	80

HCM 14

Refresher

a Out	10	14
20	18	8
b Out	40	15
30	35	45

Practice

a Out	15	21
30	27	12

b	Out	30	60
	10	80	0
c	Out	35	20
	10		
	in	5	3
d	in	5	9
	6	7	
	Out	24	

HCM 15

Refresher

a 1×4=4 **b** 6×4=24 **c** 5×4=20
d 2×4=8 **e** 9×4=36 **f** 4×4=16
g 5×4=20 **h** 3×4=12 **i** 7×4=28
j 10×4=40 **k** 8×4=32 **l** 6×4=24

Practice

Open

HCM 16

Refresher

a **b** **c**

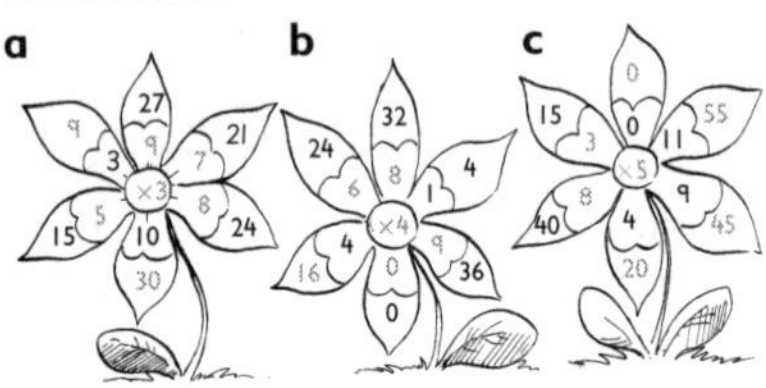

Practice

1 12 24 36 are multiples of both 3 and 4.

2a 8 **b** 40 **c** 8
d 8

HCM 17

Refresher

1a one third $\frac{1}{3}$ **b** three quarters $\frac{3}{4}$
c one third $\frac{1}{3}$ **d** half $\frac{1}{2}$
e one quarter $\frac{1}{4}$

Practice

Open

2a $\frac{1}{4}$ of 8 is 2 **b** $\frac{1}{3}$ of 9 is 3
c $\frac{1}{2}$ of 16 is 8 **d** $\frac{3}{4}$ of 12 is 9
e $\frac{2}{3}$ of 6 is 4

3 Open

HCM 18

Refresher

Answers will vary

Practice

1 Open

2a 2 **b** 2 **c** 2
d 3 **e** 2 **f** 9
g 3 **h** 6 **i** 8

HCM 19

Refresher

1a 8−3=**5** **b** 7−4=**3** **c** 6−2=**4**
d 9−3=**6** **e** 10−1=**9** **f** 15−5=**10**
g 6−3=**3** **h** 9−4=**5** **i** 17−1=**16**
j 20−2=**18**

Practice

1a 15−4=**11** **b** 18−5=**13** **c** 20−6=**14**
d 19−8=**11** **e** 13−5=**8** **f** 12−7=**5**
g 15−8=**7** **h** 11−9=**2** **i** 17−9=**8**
j 14−6=**8**

HCM 20

Refresher

Practice

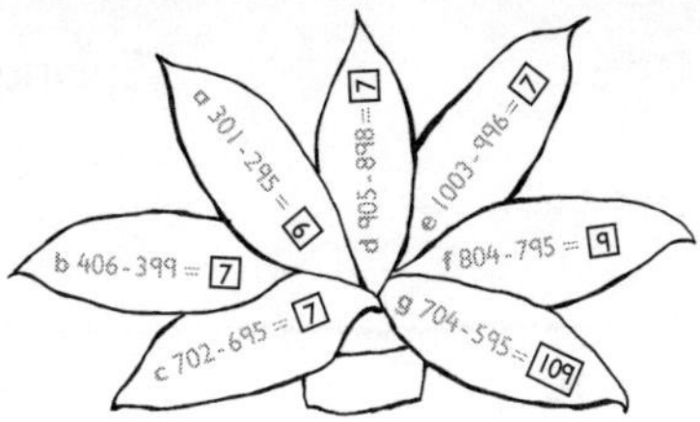

HCM 21

Refresher

1 Books 14 T-shirts 8
Dolls 6

Practice

1

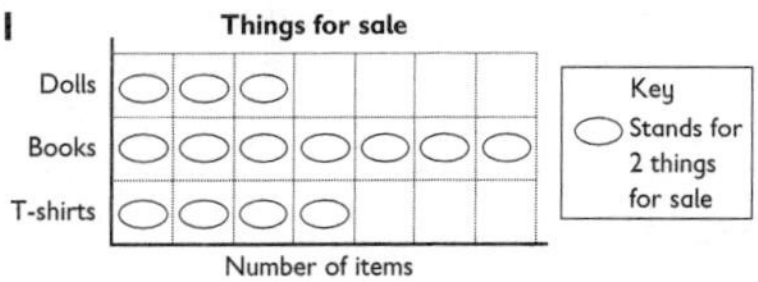

2 a 6 **b** 8 **c** books
d 8 **e** 22 **f** 28

HCM 22

Refresher

Brontosaurus 3 Tyrannosaurus 2
Stegosaurus 4 Pterodactyl 1

Practice

1

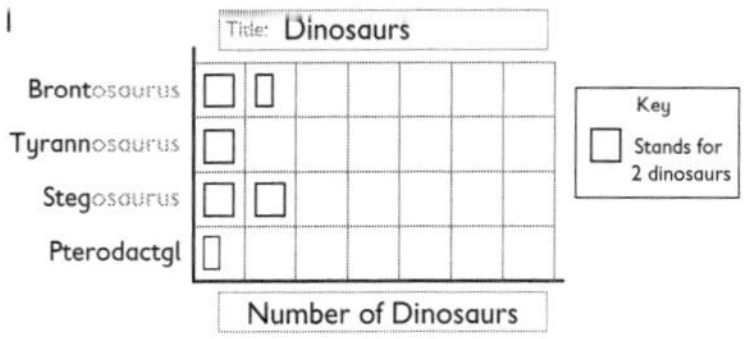

2 a 3 **b** 3
c Stegosaurus **d** 3
e 9 **f** 10

Answers

Homework Copymasters

Spring

HCM 23

Refresher

1 a 20 cm **b** 60 cm **c** 20 cm
d 90 cm **e** 70 cm

Practice

2 a 50 m **b** 10 m **c** 30 m
d 100 m **e** 70 m

3 Answers will vary

HCM 24

Answers will vary

HCM 25

Refresher

1 a 21 **b** 22 **c** 18
d 25 **e** 28 **f** 25

Practice

a 33 **b** 29 **c** 35
d 37 **e** 28 **f** 39

HCM 26

Open

HCM 27

Refresher

1 44 vegetables **2** 35 minutes

3 8 jam tarts

Practice

1 45 stickers **2** 23 more bulbs

3 2 biscuits a day

HCM 28

1

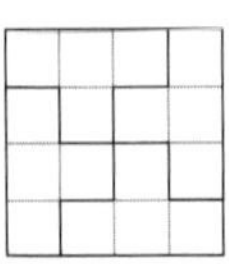

2

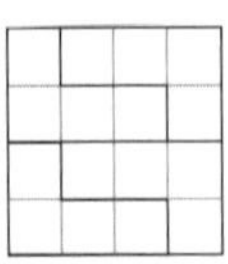

HCM 29

Open

HCM 30

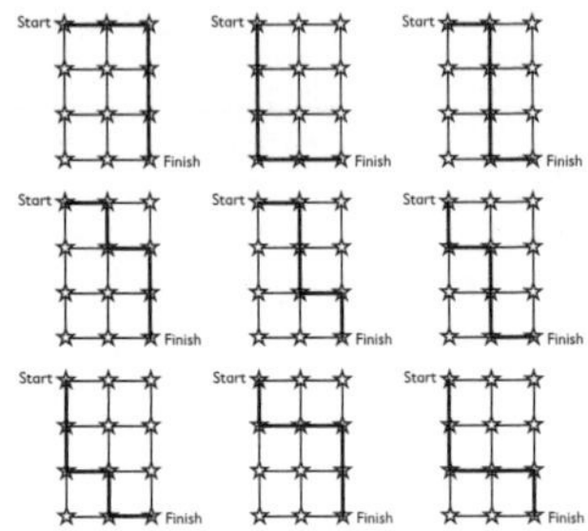

HCM 31

Open

HCM 32

Refresher

1 Dash 1 kg Dot 500 g Daisy 500 g
Dixie 500 g Dolly 1 kg

2 At dinner – time the dogs eat **1 kg 900 g** of meat altogether.

3 a The dog mixer is enough for 5 days.
b The puppy mixer is enough for 5 days.

HCM 33

Refresher

1 a

1	2	3	4	5
6	7	8	9	10
11	12	13	14	15
16	17	18	19	20
21	22	23	24	25
26	27	28	29	30
31	32	33	34	35
36	37	38	39	40
41	42	43	44	45
46	47	48	49	50

b 10 → 10 47 → **45** 16 → **15**
26 → **25** 33 → **30** 52 → **50**
41 → **40** 28 → **25** 38 → **35**

Practice

1a

1	2	3
4	5	6
7	8	9
10	11	12
13	14	15
16	17	18
19	20	21
22	23	24
25	26	27
28	29	30

b 16 → **15** 13 → **12** 11 → **9**
5 → **3** 28 → **27** 8 → **6**
24 → **24** 31 → **30** 19 → **18**

2a

1	2	3	4
5	6	7	8
9	10	11	12
13	14	15	16
17	18	19	20
21	22	23	24
25	26	27	28
29	30	31	32
33	34	35	36
37	38	39	40

b 7 → **4** 43 → **40** 30 → **28**
35 → **32** 16 → **16** 19 → **16**
21 → **20** 27 → **24** 14 → **12**

HCM 34

Refresher

2	18	6
14	8	12
10	16	4

Practice

1a

10	45	20
35	25	50
40	15	30

b

40	80	30
70	20	90
50	60	100

c

27	6	18
24	9	21
15	12	30

d

36	8	24
16	28	12
32	20	40

HCM 35

Refresher

a 16 + 21 = 37 **b** 36 + 22 = **58**
c 45 + 31 = **76** **d** 64 + 35 = **99**
e 23 + 54 = **77** **f** 72 + 26 = **98**

Practice

a 39 + 43 = **82** **b** 68 + 25 = **93**
c 76 + 24 = **100** **d** 53 + 64 = **117**
e 87 + 34 = **121** **f** 95 + 56 = **151**
g 58 + 27 = **85** **h** 84 + 77 = **161**

HCM 36

Refresher

Answers will vary

Practice

Answers will vary

HCM 37

1 20 ÷ 2 = **10** 16 ÷ 2 = **8** 40 ÷ 5 = **8**
40 ÷ 10 = **4** 30 ÷ 10 = **3** 30 ÷ 5 = **6**
18 ÷ 2 = **9** 50 ÷ 10 = **5** 15 ÷ 5 = **3**
80 ÷ 10 = **8** 50 ÷ 5 = **10** 12 ÷ 2 = **6**
14 ÷ **2** = 7 50 ÷ **5** = 10 20 ÷ **4** = 5
35 ÷ **7** = 5 **60** ÷ 10 = 6 **10** ÷ 5 = 2

Practice

1 a 6 × 10 = 60 10 × 6 = 60
60 ÷ 10 = 6 60 ÷ 6 = 10

b 5 × 8 = 40 8 × 5 = 40
40 ÷ 8 = 5 40 ÷ 5 = 8

c 3 × 8 = 24 8 × 3 = 24
24 ÷ 8 = 3 24 ÷ 3 = 8

d 4 × 7 = 28 7 × 4 = 28
28 ÷ 7 = 4 28 ÷ 4 = 7

2 a 7 (missing) 7 × 2 = 14
2 × 7 = 14 14 ÷ 2 = 7
14 ÷ 7 = 2

b 90 (missing) 9 × 10 = 90
10 × 9 = 90 90 ÷ 10 = 9
90 ÷ 9 = 10

c 6 (missing) 6 × 5 = 30
5 × 6 = 30 30 ÷ 5 = 6
30 ÷ 6 = 5

d 7 (missing) 3×7=21
7×3=21 21÷7=3
21÷3=7

HCM 38

Refresher

1 a 20–**40** 50–**100**
100–**200** 40–**80**

b 16 – **32** 25–**50**
65 – **130** 19 – **38**

c 400–**800** 50–**100**
30–**60** 120–**240**

Practice

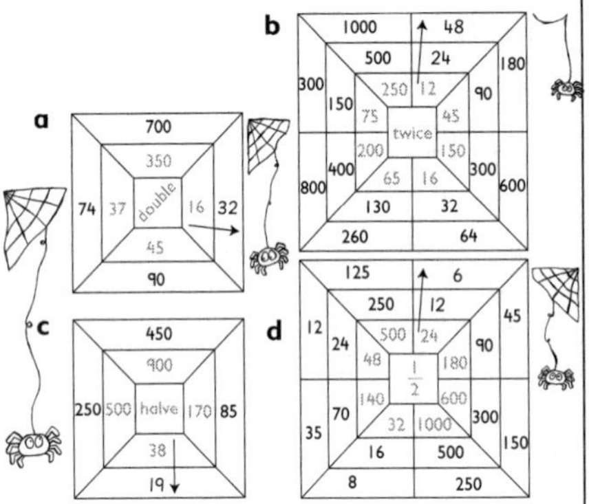

HCM 39

Answers will vary

HCM 40

Refresher

Answers will vary

Practice

1 a $\frac{3}{10}$ **b** $\frac{1}{10}$ **c** $\frac{4}{10}$
d $\frac{2}{10}$ **e** $\frac{5}{10}$

2 a $\frac{2}{10}$ **b** $\frac{4}{10}$ **c** $\frac{1}{10}$
d $\frac{3}{10}$ **e** $\frac{5}{10}$

HCM 41

Refresher

1 footballs 10 rackets 6
bats 6 goggles 14

Practice

1

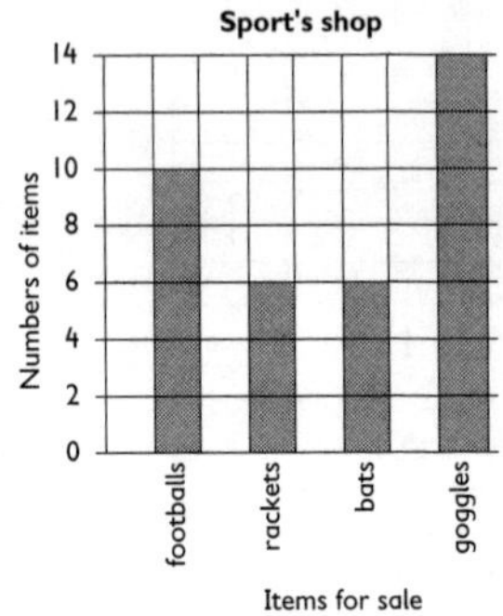

a goggles **b** 4 **c** 3

HCM 42

Refresher

Spots	Tally	Total
2	III	3
3	~~IIII~~ IIII	9
4	~~IIII~~ I	6
5	IIII	4
6	I	1

Practice

1

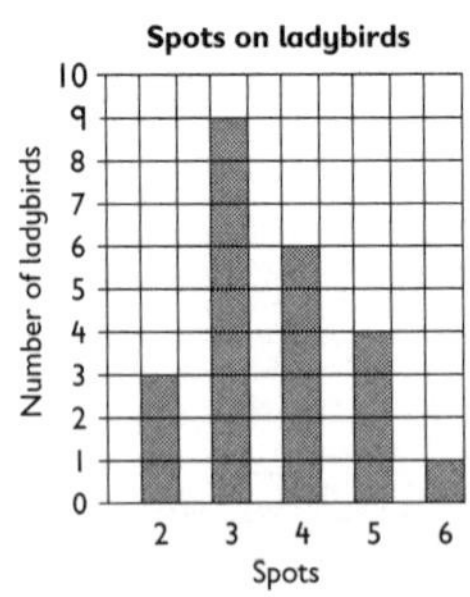

1 a There is only one ladybird with 6 spots.
b 4 spots
c 5 ladybirds have more than 4 spots.

Answers

Homework Copymasters

Summer

HCM 43

Refresher

1 a 800 g b 300 g c 100 g
d 700 g e 100 g

Practice

1 a 600 kg b 200 kg c 400 kg
d 0 kg e 200 kg

2 Answers will vary

HCM 44

Refresher

a 39 b 95 c 33
d 37 e 78 f 56
g 7 h 7 i 34
j 14 k 24 l 32

Practice

a 81 b 11 c 32
d 78 e 57 f 55
g 78 h 94 i 97
j 87 k 97 l 36

HCM 45

Refresher

1 a 50 b 140 c 60
d 90 e 150 f 60
g 100 h 150 I 20
j 120 k 40 l 20
m 110 n 40 o 20

Practice

1 a 92 b 118 c 90
d 59 e 121 f 50
g 77 h 136 i 70
j 116 k 134 l 50
m 112 n 145 o 80

2 a 240 + 60 = 300 b 630 + 70 = 700
c 270 + 30 = 300 d 780 + 20 = 800
e 310 + 90 = 400 f 550 + 50 = 600
g 490 + 10 = 500 h 990 + 10 = 1000
i 540 + 60 = 600 j 830 + 70 – 900

HCM 46

Answers will vary

HCM 47

Refresher

a 31 + 25

	3	1	
	2	5	+
units		6	
tens	5	0	
answer	5	6	

b 42 + 34

	4	2	
	3	4	+
units		6	
	7	0	
	7	6	

c 62 + 27

	6	2	
	2	7	+
units		9	
tens	8	0	
	8	9	

d 13 + 26

	1	3	
	2	6	+
units		9	
tens	3	0	
answer	3	9	

e 52 + 17

	5	2	
	1	7	+
units		9	
tens	6	0	
	6	9	

f 43 + 36

	4	3	
	3	6	+
units		9	
tens	7	0	
	7	9	

Practice

a 137 + 42

	1	3	7	
		4	2	+
units			9	
tens		7	0	
hundreds	1	0	0	
answer	1	7	9	

b 153 + 25

	1	5	3	
		2	5	
units			8	
tens		7	0	
hundreds	1	0	0	
answer	1	7	8	

c 146 + 33

	1	4	6	
		3	3	
units			9	
tens		7	0	
hundreds	1	0	0	
answer	1	7	9	

d 139 + 46

	1	3	9	
		4	6	+
units		1	5	
tens		7	0	
hundreds	1	0	0	
answer	1	8	5	

e 162 + 29

	1	6	2	
		2	9	
units		1	1	
tens		8	0	
hundreds	1	0	0	
answer	1	9	1	

f 155 + 38

	1	5	5	
		3	8	
units		1	3	
tens		8	0	
hundreds	1	0	0	
answer	1	9	3	

HCM 48

Refresher

Answers will vary

Practice

1 A full kettle holds $1\frac{1}{2}$ litres or 1500 millilitres

2 The teapot holds 800 ml
There are 700 ml left in the kettle

3 The cup holds 200 ml
There are 600 ml left in the teapot

4 The teapot will fill 4 cups

5 She can fill 2 mugs
200 ml of tea is left in the teapot

HCM 49

Refresher

Answers will vary

Practice

Answers will vary

HCM 50

Refresher

Open

Practice

Open

HCM 51

Pattern should **reflect** exactly across mirror line.

HCM 52

Refresher

1 a multiples of 5:
450 15 310 85 125 225 20

b multiples of 2:
216 80 22 138 16 164 448

c multiples of 10:
20 80 50 460 100 130 270

Practice

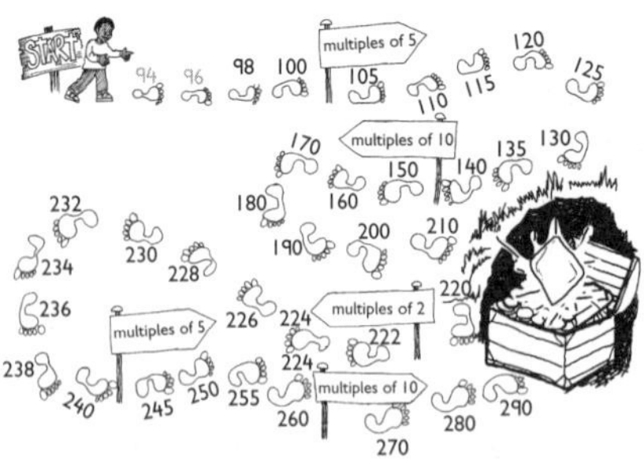

HCM 53

Refresher

1 a 16 **b** 19 **c** 20
d 30 **e** 22 **f** 60
g 63

Practice

a Total = 12

7	2	3
0	4	8
5	6	1

b Total = 18

3	8	7
10	6	2
5	4	9

c Total = 15

4	3	8
9	5	1
2	7	6

d Total = 30

13	6	11
8	10	12
9	14	7

e Total = 27

8	7	12
13	9	5
6	11	10

f Total = 75

26	21	28
27	25	23
22	29	24

HCM 54

Refresher

1 a 13 ÷ 3 = 4 (r1) **b** 22 ÷ 10 = 2 (r2)
c 17 ÷ 5 = 3 (r2) **d** 14 ÷ 4 = 3 (r2)
e 11 ÷ 2 = 5 (r1) **f** 23 ÷ 5 = 4 (r3)

Practice

1 a Think… 3 × 5 = 15
So…… 16 ÷ 5 = 3 (r1)

b Think… 2 × 10 = 20
So…… 23 ÷ 10 = 2 (r3)

c Think… 3 × 10 = 30
So…… 32 ÷ 3 = 10 (r2)

d Think… 6 × 4 = 24
So…… 26 ÷ 4 = 6 (r2)

e Think… 7 × 5 = 45
So…… 38 ÷ 5 = 7 (r3)

f Think… 9 × 3 = 27
So…… 29 ÷ 3 = 9 (r2)

HCM 55

Refresher

1 a 3 3 8 8 10 6
b 7 7 10 8 6 5
c 9 3 3 10 10 10

Practice

1 a 20 ÷ 4 = 5 Each side is 5 cm
b 10 ÷ 5 = 2 It costs £2 per ride
c 23 ÷ 5 = 2 5 tiles have a pattern
d 16 ÷ 3 = 5 (r1) 1 sweet is left over
e 33 ÷ 5 = 6 (r3) 3 balls are left over

HCM 56

Refresher

1 a $23\times2=46$ $20\times2=40$
$3\times2=6$ $40+6=46$

b $2\times24=48$ $2\times20=40$
$2\times4=8$ $40+8=48$

c $3\times32=96$ $3\times30=90$
$3\times2=6$ $90+6=96$

d $3\times13=39$ $3\times10=30$
$3\times3=9$ $30+9=39$

e $4\times12=48$ $4\times10=40$
$4\times2=8$ $40+8=48$

f $5\times11=55$ $5\times10=50$
$5\times1=5$ $50+5=55$

g $3\times23=69$ $3\times20=60$
$3\times3=9$ $60+9=69$

h $33\times2=66$ $30\times2=60$
$3\times2=6$ $60+6=66$

i $11\times4=44$ $10\times4=40$
$1\times4=4$ $40+4=44$

Practice

1 a 48   **b** 46   **c** 88
d 30   **e** 44   **f** 86
g 99   **h** 68   **i** 88
j 50   **k** 66   **l** 36

HCM 57

Refresher

1 a $\frac{1}{4}$ **b** $\frac{3}{4}$ **c** $1\frac{1}{2}$
d $2\frac{1}{4}$ **e** $4\frac{3}{4}$

2 $\frac{1}{4}, \frac{1}{2}, \frac{3}{4}, (1), 1\frac{1}{4}, 1\frac{1}{2}, 1\frac{3}{4}, (2), 2\frac{1}{4}, 2\frac{1}{2}, 2\frac{3}{4}, (3), 3\frac{1}{4}, 3\frac{1}{2}, 3\frac{3}{4}$

Practice

1 a $\frac{3}{4}$ **b** $\frac{1}{2}$ **c** $1\frac{3}{4}$ **d** $3\frac{1}{2}$
2 a $\frac{3}{4}$ **b** $1\frac{1}{8}$ **c** $3\frac{1}{2}$ **d** 1
3 a $1\frac{1}{4}$ **b** $1\frac{3}{4}$ **c** 2   **d** 4

HCM 58

Refresher

1 a 40   **b** 30
c 10   **d** 25

Practice

1 a 16   **b** 12 or 13   **c** 24   **d** 7 or 8
2 a 50   **b** 32   **c** 60   **d** 48
3 a 21 or 22   **b** 7 or 8   **c** 34   **d** 52

HCM 59

Refresher

a	46	55	67
b	13	22	35
c	800	500	600
d	400	100	200
e	162	134	179
f	67	85	26

Practice

a	121	108	114
b	86	95	78
c	1100	1400	1500
d	800	600	900
e	724	618	856
f	171	393	757

HCM 60

Refresher

July

S	*M*	*T*	*W*	*Th*	*F*	*S*
				1	2	3
4	5	6	7	8	9	10
11	12	13	14	15	16	17
18	19	20	21	22	23	24
25	26	27	28	29	30	31

Practice

2 a 2, 4, 6, 8, 10, 12, 14, 16, 18, 20, 22, 24, 26, 28, 30
b 3, 6, 9, 12, 15, 18, 21, 24, 27, 30
c 7, 14, 21, 28

3 a For the even numbers – should form a diagonal pattern across the calendar
b For the threes – will form two diagonals across the calendar
c For the sevens – appear in a line going down – all occur on a Wednesday

4 6, 12, 14, 18, 21, 24, 28, 30